Jesus of Nazareth

My Lord

Héctor E. Hoppe

Translated by
Pamela Bridgehouse

3558 S. Jefferson Ave., St. Louis, MO 63118-3968 U.S.A.

Manufactured in the United States of America.

Original title in Spanish: *Jesús de Nazaret, mi Señor.* Copyright © 2003 Editorial Concordia.

Translator: Pam Bridgehouse

Manufactured in the United States of America

Library of Congress Cataloging-in-Publication Data

Hoppe, Héctor E.
[Jesús de Nazaret, mi Señor. English]
Jesus of Nazareth, my Lord / Héctor E. Hoppe.
p. cm.
ISBN 978-0-7586-3852-6
1. Jesus Christ--Person and offices--Biblical teaching. I. Title.

BT203.H66513 2013
232--dc23

2012035021

1 2 3 4 5 6 7 8 9 10 21 20 19 18 17 16 15 14 13 12

To my parents,
Juan and María Cristina,
who taught me to recognize in
Jesus of Nazareth, my Lord.

Contents

Chapter 1

Part 1:
A Death with Significance

"Marcelo: Dedicated his life to help the needy."
"Here lies María Elena, tireless teacher."

These brief words, carved in stone or on metal, help friends and families remember the purpose of their loved ones' lives.

We don't know if there was a phrase summarizing Jesus' life on His tomb. We do know that it was sealed and that the Pharisees and the chief priests asked the Roman authorities to post guards outside the tomb, suspecting the disciples might steal His body (Matthew 27:62–66). Although Jesus' existence changed many people's lives, His death and resurrection changed the course of all humanity and the relationship between mankind and God. Someone might sum up Jesus' life this way: "He dedicated His life to healing the sick" or "He will be remembered for His compassion for the poor and outcast."

The New Testament certainly affirms this truth:

> While we were still sinners, Christ died for us. (Romans 5:8)

The author of the Letter to the Hebrews is even more explicit regarding Jesus' death and its consequences:

> Christ was sacrificed once to take away the sins of many people. (Hebrews 9:28)

It can almost be said that Jesus came to die, or that He dedicated His life to preparing for His death. When we search through the Gospels, we are astounded to see how many times Jesus makes reference to His death. When the disciples criticized a woman for pouring an expensive perfume over Jesus' head, the Lord said to them:

> When she poured this perfume on My body, she did it to prepare Me for burial. (Matthew 26:12)

Matthew takes several opportunities to make reference to Jesus announcing His own death. Just before His triumphal entry into Jerusalem, Jesus says to His disciples:

> The Son of Man will be betrayed to the chief priests and the teachers of the law. They will condemn Him to death and will turn Him over to the Gentiles to be mocked and flogged and crucified. On the third day He will be raised to life! (Matthew 20:18–19)

What's this all about? A death planned in such rich detail? "Mocked and flogged and crucified"? What kind of a death was that?

The author of Hebrews insists that Jesus' death meant expiation, a sacrificial payment for sins (Hebrews 10:10–12). From the beginning of the Christian Church, the cross has been one of the major symbols of our faith, because it is the altar where the Lamb of God was sacrificed. That cross that we see every day as a decoration, in churches, or at the head of a bed is intimately related to a gold plate about forty inches long by twenty-eight inches wide described in the Book of Exodus as an "atonement cover" (Exodus 25:17). This gold plate was the top that covered the ark of the Testimony. The Law of God was placed inside this ark and was covered by the "atonement" (v. 21). The Book of Leviticus explains the functions of the ark of the Testimony and especially the atonement. In Leviticus 16:14–15, God tells Moses that the priest needs to enter the sanctuary and sprinkle the atonement with blood; He adds (v. 34) that this is an order that the sons of Israel must follow to make atonement once a year for all the sins of Israel. By this we understand that Jesus of Nazareth was born to be the gold plate that, with His blood, would cover the Law that accuses us. The Bible often refers to Jesus as the "propitiation" for our sins. In other words, Jesus and His blood covered the Law that condemned me. Paul establishes this when he writes to the Romans:

> [We] are justified freely by His grace through the redemption that came by Christ Jesus. God presented Him as a sacrifice of atonement, through faith in His blood. (Romans 3:24–25)

Christians of Jewish origin who knew the history of the ark of the Testimony and of the atonement and its function understood well that in order for the atonement to be effective, it needed to be sprinkled with blood. In other words, there was no forgiveness of sins without sacrifice, death, or the sprinkling of the blood over the atonement. Although this scene was celebrated just once a year, it was sufficiently strong to be emblazoned in the memory of the children of Israel. When a child asked his parents why the priest entered the tabernacle with blood, still warm from a male goat or a calf, to sprinkle over and in front of the atonement, he received an answer that included the mercy of God, the sacrifice and death of an innocent one, and the redemption or liberation of his people. These three aspects are still known today. It was God's mercy that sent the innocent Lamb to be sacrificed and to die for the liberation of His people. The apostle John sums it up like this:

> This is love: . . . He loved us and sent His Son as an atoning sacrifice for our sins. (1 John 4:10)

The blood was a vital element in the religious ceremonies of Israel. Jesus began to shed His blood when, in agony, "His sweat was like drops of blood" (Luke 22:44), and John in his Gospel carefully records the moment when "one of the soldiers pierced Jesus' side with a spear, bringing a sudden flow of blood and water" (John 19:34).

Today, every time we approach the altar to participate in Holy Communion, Jesus sprinkles us with His blood, so that God might not see the Law that condemns us, and so that we might experience the forgiveness that delivers us.

It is interesting that many times we pray, "Lord, have mercy" (literally, 'be my atonement'), and by this we implore the favor of God. This is the way the tax collector prayed in Luke 18:13: "God, have mercy on me [literally, "be my atonement"], a sinner." If we apply the figure of the atonement from the Old Testament to this prayer, we understand that this sinner was asking God to pour blood over him to wash away his sins, or for God to place the atonement over him so the Law might not reveal his sins. When we pray that God might have mercy on us, that we might be "atoned for," we are asking Him to cover us with the blood of the Lamb, Jesus.

Jesus was born and lived to pour out His blood. Only by understanding the profound significance and purpose of His death will we be able to understand His life and ministry. His death on the altar of the cross gave significance to His life.

Read Exodus 25:10–25 and Leviticus 16:1–34.

Think about these outstanding points:

- Atonement
- Sacrifice
- Blood
- Pardon

Reflect on how these Old Testament rites relate to Jesus.

Part 2:
Perfectly Planned

Someone who plans ahead is more likely to make better use of their time and energy. That's one of the benefits of planning in any area of life. The one who makes plans knows what he wants and concentrates his efforts in order to reach his goals. Planning arises from the dreams and expectations one has in life.

For example, it is very common that family planning begins long before actually establishing a family. Couples like to "dream," to talk about how many children they would like to have, how they will be educated, what school they would like them to attend, and so forth. But the truth is that things don't always work out according to plan. Sometimes there are surprises. People expecting a child could have twins, or they could be surprised by having a child when they planned to wait. A couple may want a boy but have a girl. Some couples who want to have at least one child come to find they cannot have any.

Mary and Joseph were engaged, and surely, as pious children of God, they wanted to be blessed with many children. Remember that for the Israelites, having children was a sign of divine blessing. Luke relates, for example, that Mary's elderly relative Elizabeth, of the region of Judea, had never been able to have children. Sadly, Elizabeth and her husband, Zechariah, had to suffer the absence of this blessing throughout their entire married life. On the other hand, Mary and Joseph surely anxiously awaited the time when they could fill the house with children. But God had other plans and surprised Elizabeth and Zechariah by allowing them to bring into the world the greatest of all prophets: John the Baptist. The angel Gabriel, who announced John's coming to Zechariah, also surprised Mary with a change of plans.

The birth of Jesus was not a mistake committed by Mary and Joseph, but the culmination of God's meticulous and elaborate plan. Beginning with Genesis 3:15, in which God makes a promise to Adam and Eve that He would send a Savior after they fell into sin, and throughout Scripture, we find many prophecies that speak of Jesus and His work.

In order to understand that God took our salvation very seriously and planned it intricately, it is important to take into account that over the course of many years, He kept on revealing information about the Messiah to His people. Jeremiah, in one of the most important messianic passages of his book, writes:

> "The days are coming," declares the LORD, "when I will raise up to David a righteous Branch, a King who will reign wisely and do what is just and right in the land. In His days Judah will be saved and Israel will live in safety. This is the name by which He will be called: The LORD Our Righteousness." (Jeremiah 23:5–6)

In just a few words Jeremiah gives us important information about God's plans. First of all, it is God Himself who "will raise up to David a righteous Branch." Jesus didn't come because of human will but because God had established it from the beginning. It follows that He will not come from just any family, but from the branch of King David.

Jeremiah describes the Messiah's work by explaining that "He will practice justice," and that justice will produce a fundamental change in the lives of the people from Judah and Israel: they will live in peace and trust. He will be named "The LORD Our Righteousness."

We should note that in his Gospel, Matthew includes the words of the angel when he appeared to Joseph in a dream:

> Joseph son of David, do not be afraid to take Mary home as your wife. . . . She will give birth to a son, and you are to give Him the name Jesus, because He will save His people from their sins. (Matthew 1:20–21)

Now Joseph could begin to connect the information given him by the angel with the prophecies from the Scriptures. Perhaps he couldn't make the connection immediately. Perhaps only with time could Joseph observe how the words of the angel were deeply rooted in Jeremiah's prophecy and in so many other writings in the Law and the Prophets. Perhaps one of the outstanding points of both passages is that God insists that the child will be called "Jesus," or, from Jeremiah's words, "Our Righteousness." Justice and salvation are intimately connected. In fact, some translations of the Old Testament use the terms "salvation" and "justice" interchangeably without distinction, because even then we were already saved by the Messiah's work of righteousness. All of this is tied to the name's meaning. The angels' words "You will name Him Jesus" are vitally important for understanding the work of the Messiah. In the language of the Bible, the name is tied to the being of the person. The Messiah needed to be named *Jesus*, or "our justice," because in the divine plan, it was He who would save us from our sins and make us just before God.

Perhaps before all this took place, Mary and Joseph were thinking of names for their children, but God had other plans. Now they had something more important to think about. For Joseph, it was not easy to take a pregnant woman for his wife and give a name and a home to her child. An angel was needed to convince Joseph that Mary had been chosen by God to provide salvation for humanity through His Son. The Bible tells us that Mary was a pious woman and that she complied with the change of plans that God brought to her life, saying:

> "May it be to me as you have said." Then the angel left her. (Luke 1:38)

Thanks to Mary and Joseph's faith and dedication, Jesus was born, grew up, carried out His ministry, died, and rose. Note that on the same day He rose from the dead, Jesus is put into contact with some of His disciples:

> Beginning with Moses and all the Prophets, He explained to them what was said in all the Scriptures concerning Himself. (Luke 24:27)

Jesus knew that the Old Testament testified to His coming and His work, and He didn't miss the opportunity to make this known to His disciples.

It is no wonder, then, that Matthew begins his Gospel with the genealogy of Jesus, beginning with the patriarch Abraham. Matthew wanted to show his readers (including us today) that when God gave a son to Abraham, He was planning that through this lineage, many generations later, the Savior of the world would be born. God was planning the same thing when He gave sons to Isaac and Jacob and so on until the arrival of Joseph, Jesus' earthly father. Nothing was by chance. Everything was perfectly planned.

Read Isaiah 42:1–9.

This is one of the passages in which the work of the Servant of God is described in detail.

Think about the outstanding points of this passage, and describe how Jesus' ministry is characterized.

Read Isaiah 52:13–53:1–12.

Relate what Isaiah says in this passage to the passion and atonement of Jesus.

Part 3:
In Jesus, God Has a Plan and a Purpose for Me

God's love for me is revealed in the way He carefully planned the incarnation of His Son. Even from the beginning, the Bible says that God would take my salvation on Himself. In Genesis 3 there is a verse that divides the Bible into two important parts. The verse describes the sentence and the promise that God makes in the Garden of Eden. God says to Satan:

> I will put enmity between you and the woman, and between your offspring and hers; He will crush your head, and you will strike His heal. (Genesis 3:15)

With this verse that promises the coming of the Savior, the division is marked between the story of my creation and the story of my redemption. It only took two and half chapters out of the whole Bible to establish God as my Creator and Father. As for the rest of the hundreds of chapters beginning with Genesis 3:15, they are the history of my salvation in Christ Jesus. How many prophecies, histories, and experiences God made to reveal to me the way of salvation! The story of my liberation is filled with accounts that God describes in rich detail so that I, and people from all times, might have no doubt about the attention He dedicates to us.

Why does Isaiah describe the suffering of Jesus so extensively? So I can have consolation knowing that someone took my place when it was time for punishment and suffering. Why did Matthew write such a long genealogy in the first chapter of his Gospel? So that I might realize that the Savior God who was sent to set me free from my sins was not born by chance, but was carefully planned. Throughout the whole Bible, God guides me so that I might put my faith in Jesus, His Son, so that my life—and death—will have meaning!

Was I born by chance? No! I did not come into this world without the consent of my Father Creator. Has God put me in this world for a purpose? He certainly has! No life is useless or without meaning to God. He had a well-defined plan for Zechariah and Elizabeth. Although they did not have a child until they were old, it was worth the wait to see the purpose of God fulfilled through the birth of John the Baptist.

Knowing that God has a plan for my life gives me much joy and satisfaction. I don't always see His purpose clearly in certain things that happen to me. Generally I realize, when I look back, that all the things that happened to me and the things God guided me to do truly included a plan for my well-being and a testimony of His love to others.

If God has a plan for my life, He also has one for my death; and if God has a purpose for my life, He also has a purpose for my death. It is God's plan that through my death, I will truly be set free from all impurity and will be able to enjoy abundantly the freedom to which I was called at my Baptism. God planned a glorious resurrection for me and a place together with Him and all believers, where life will be much different than it is now because:

> Never again will they hunger; never again will they thirst. . . . And God will wipe away every tear from their eyes. (Revelation 7:16–17)

As a human being used to certain routines, I don't like it when plans get changed. I'm not always prepared for surprises. I like stability, and I think life would be much easier if everything went according to my plans. God doesn't think so. I'm constantly experiencing changes, and when I happily accept them, I discover that God permits me to see opportunities for service and blessing that I wouldn't have seen in any other way.

What doesn't change is my sinful condition. I can grow and mature and manage my moods and relationships better, but deep down, self-centeredness, envy, and many other sins begin to appear, showing me that I can't do it on my own. I need Jesus. The other thing that doesn't change is the covenant, the blood of the Lamb poured out to cleanse me from my sins. God's attitude of looking after me every time I don't live according to His purposes doesn't change. His Word doesn't change, and His promise to stay with me forever, even through all eternity, doesn't change.

It isn't easy for me to imitate Joseph's attitude, or that of Mary. They were both obedient to God's instructions and freely submitted themselves to His will. I don't imagine that God would have chosen Joseph if he hadn't been able to be a good father, and I don't believe He would have chosen Mary to raise His Son if she would not have been a virtuous mother. I would like to reach the level of obedience and submission of Jesus' earthly parents. Their example inspires me.

I always read the Scriptures. I like the Old Testament, with its stories of battles and champions of the faith. God often surprises me by revealing something new to me, especially in His attitude toward mankind. The prophecies of Isaiah and Jeremiah impress me with the exactitude and details they put into the minds and hearts of the people of God. It brings me comfort to discover in the Scriptures how exactly God planned for my salvation, my well-being, and my joy. I am reassured by how quickly God reacted to the sin of Adam and Eve, and how, after the judgment, He immediately made the promise of the Seed that would be born (Jesus) to crush the head of the evil one (Genesis 3:15). God doesn't lose any time before consoling His children. He never has. He never will.

Find your favorite Old Testament passages that describe the Messiah.

How do you understand God's purpose for your life?

Chapter 2

Part 1: *The Strategic Geographic Location of Palestine*

Throughout the history of the Church, there have been people who believed religion to be something exclusively spiritual. The physical and corporal aspects were not well regarded. Although the Bible says that as Christians, we need to be apart from the world, the physical aspect, specifically the earthly aspect, is of great importance for the development of the Christian faith. Just look at all the "earthly" movement found in the Holy Scriptures in relation to the formation and establishment of the people of God. Many times, the Old Testament cites the words "Promised Land." The "Promised Land" was not a heavenly land or a spiritual space, but rather a strip of land located in a very specific place on planet earth. It was a physical space with important characteristics so that God could plant there, through His chosen people, the work of salvation for humankind.

The story of the Promised Land begins with the unique call of Abram. First Abram left Ur of the Chaldeans with his father and other relatives. He headed north between the Tigris and Euphrates rivers, arriving in Haran. He remained there until his father's death (Genesis 11:31–32), and later continued on toward his final destination, the place God had promised to give to his descendants: Canaan.

Abram's journey can be seen on Map 1 (p. 25). Note that it was impossible to travel by means of the transportation of those times directly from Ur to the Promised Land through the desert. Abram, his relatives, servants, and animals all needed water to stay alive. This area of the great rivers was known as the Fertile Crescent. The waters made the land fit for planting and supporting livestock. The international roads were traced along the valleys formed by these rivers, and along these rivers the great empires of antiquity were established: Babylon, Assyria, and Egypt.

Observe where Canaan and its small Jordan River are located: in the midst of great world powers and in the corridor of international commerce. This area was always coveted by the surrounding powers, for whoever had control over the international trade routes could flourish both politically and commercially. On the map, the small Jordan River can be seen in relation to the Tigris, Euphrates, and the Nile. We can also see how small the Promised Land is compared with the neighboring empires. But despite its small size, it was of vital importance because it was the only route for commercial and military caravans. At the time of Jesus' birth, the Romans also used this territory for their commercial traffic and political strategies, navigating the Mediterranean, then entering Caesarea in order to pass through Canaan to reach their destinations.

"The Way of the Sea" is the name of a network of international roads that spread through Canaan from end to end (see Map 2, p. 26). Southwest of the Canaanite territory there is a section with five valleys, known as the "Valleys of Shefela" (see Map 3, p. 27). To the west of those valleys, on the Mediterranean coast, is where the Philistines lived. The Philistines were descendants of the Phoenicians who arrived in Canaan around the same time that the people of Israel began to occupy the territory from the east, passing through the Jordan River on the heights of Jericho.

These two civilizations confronted each other constantly, each trying to maintain sovereignty over the region. The valleys permitted access between The Way of the Patriarchs, a road across the mountains, and The Way of the Sea, which ran along the Mediterranean coast. In the middle of this region to the east is the Elah Valley, in which the famous battle between David and Goliath took place. Had the Philistines won, they would have been easily able to go up from Gath—one of the cities where they were settled—and from there to Bethlehem and on to Jerusalem, thus dominating the most important city in Canaan, along with its main roads. But thanks to God, Jesus' ancestor David not only understood political and military strategies, but he also completely trusted in God as the source of all power. After David defeated Goliath, the Philistines retreated and stayed in the cities of Gath and Ekron, located on The Way of the Sea. All the international commercial traffic passed through those two cities, so it didn't take long for word of the Hebrews' triumph over the Philistines to reach every corner, thus fulfilling David's prophecy:

> And the whole world will know that there is a God in Israel. (1 Samuel 17:46)

The battle between David and Goliath, added to the accounts of other battles and events that took place in Canaan during the times of the Old and New Testaments, made Palestine a testing ground for the people of God. Deuteronomy describes the Promised Land and the covenant of God with His people:

> Observe the commands of the Lord your God, walking in His ways and revering Him. For the Lord your God is bringing you into a good land—a land with streams and pools of water, with springs flowing in the valleys and hills; a land with wheat and barley, vines and fig trees, pomegranates, olive oil and honey; a land where bread will not be scarce and you will lack nothing; a land where the rocks are iron and you can dig copper out of the hills. (Deuteronomy 8:6–9)

If such a fruitful and abundant land, with natural springs ideal for pasturing flocks, and being so strategically located, was changed into a testing ground with much suffering and slavery instead of a blessed inheritance, it was because God's chosen people didn't want to understand that the blessings of God were tied to the fulfillment of the Commandments He had given to them on Mount Sinai.

For centuries, Canaan was the testing ground for the people of God. The time of Jesus' birth was no exception. The Roman Empire had occupied Palestine since 64 BC. Although the people had certain freedoms to worship God in the temple and to celebrate the chief annual festivals, in reality, they were slaves in their own territory. They suffered foreign invasion, trampling on their civil rights, and the imposition of extremely high taxes. Above all, the national pride was wounded. God's people were held captive by a pagan empire. When would the Messiah, the Liberator, come? When would Canaan stop being the land of trial and foreign domination? These questions rose among the people every time there was an uprising in the temple at Jerusalem, a massacre in Galilee, or an insurrection against the Romans during one of the chief feasts.

Read Deuteronomy 8:1–10.

- Reflect on the goodness of the Promised Land described in the Bible passage in relation to the life of slavery the people of God had lived in Egypt.
- Reflect on the relationship between obedience to the Commandments and the promise of blessing in the land of Canaan.
- Observe the strategic location of Palestine in relation to the large neighboring empires. Think about how the story from 1 Samuel 17 (David and Goliath) is a good example of how the strategic geographic location was key in spreading the story of the battle.

Map 1

Mediterranean Sea
Black Sea
Caspian Sea
Nile
Caesarea
Canaan
Jerusalem
Jordan
Euphrates
Haran
Tigris
Ur
N

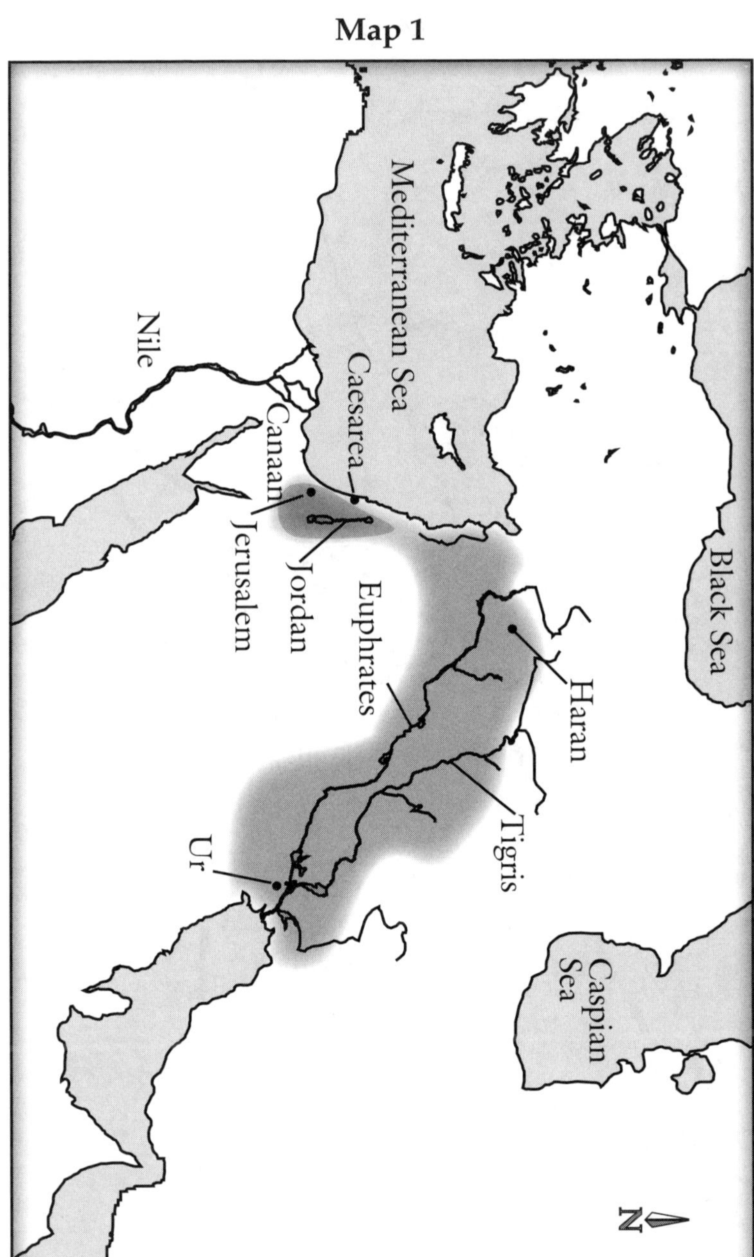

Map 2

The Way of the Sea
N
Toward Rome
Toward Damascus
Sea of Galilee
Caesarea by the Sea
The Way of the Sea
Mediterranean Sea
Jordan River
Route of the King
Jerusalem
Bethlehem
Dead Sea
Toward Egypt
Toward Petra

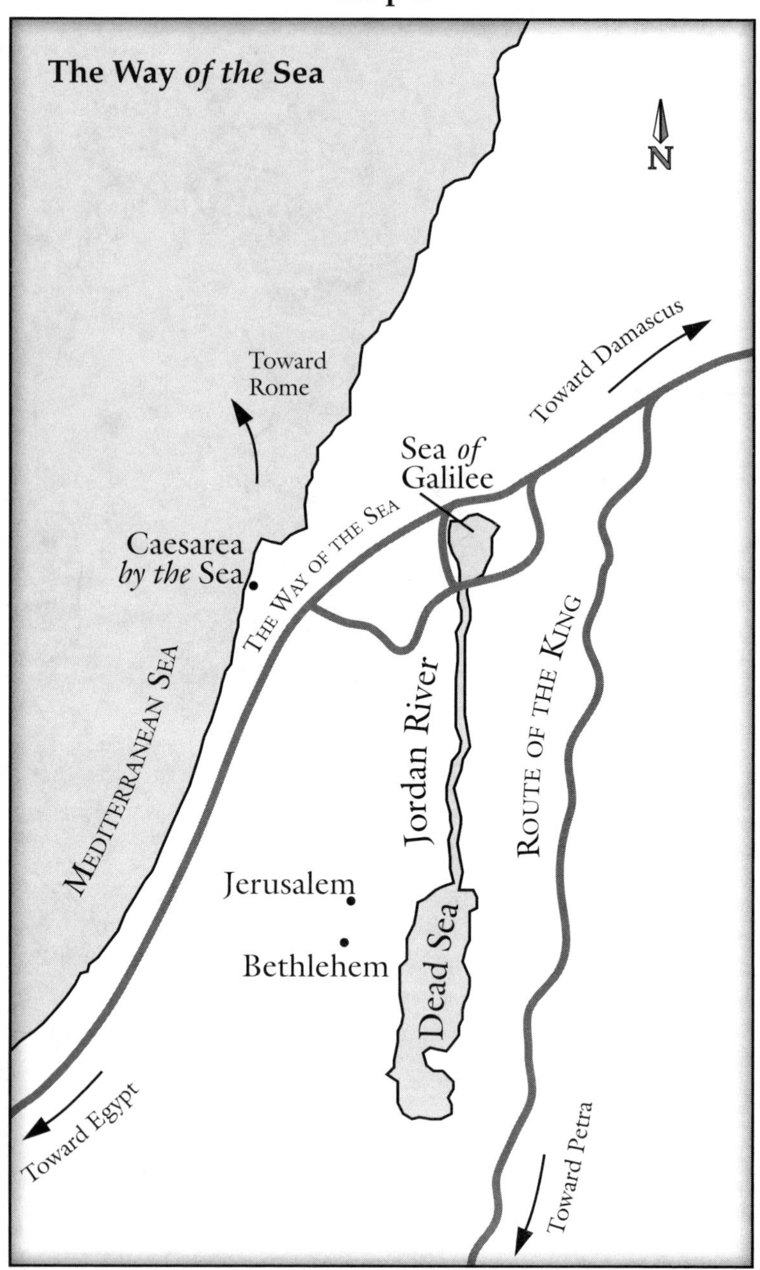

Map 3

Valleys of Shefela
N
Toward Rome and Assyria
The Way of the Sea
Ekron
Gath
Azekah
Sochoh
Toward Egypt
Jerusalem
Bethlehem
Way of the Patriarchs
Toward Jordan and the Persian Gulf

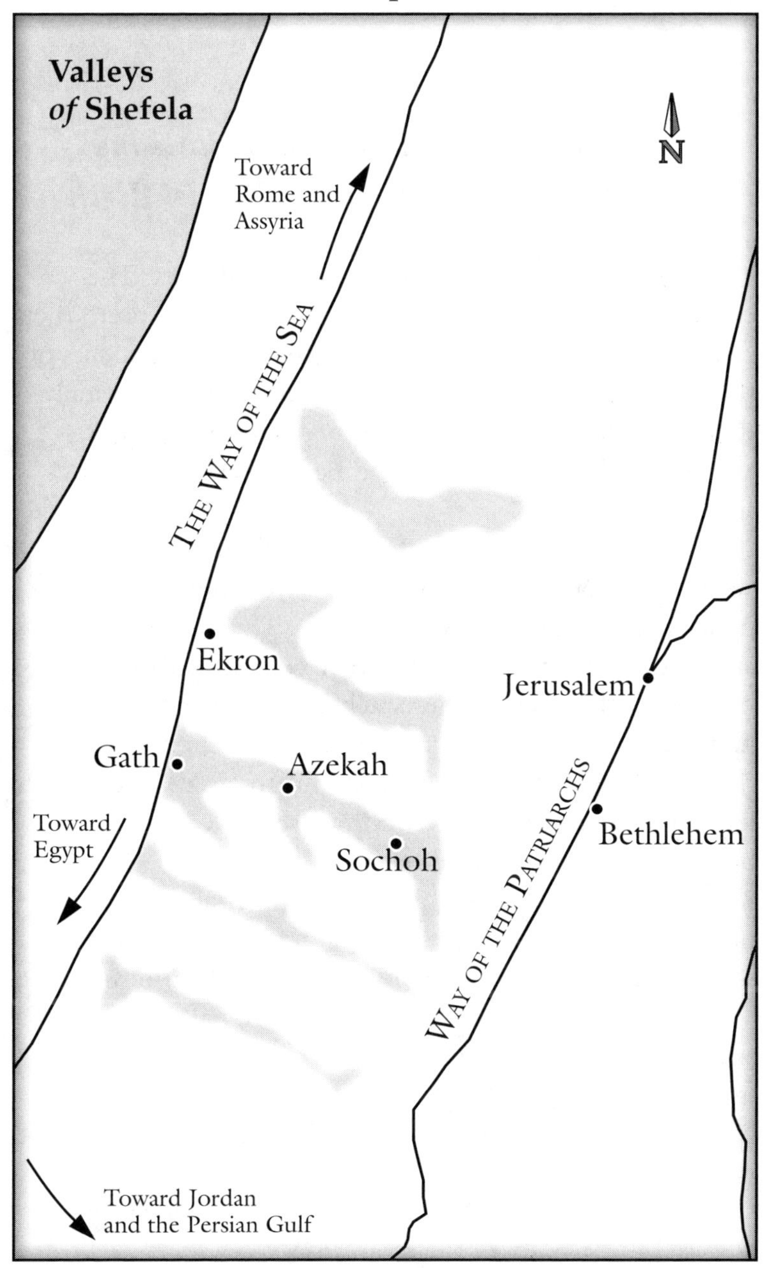

Part 2:
The Political and Social Situations in Palestine at the Time of Jesus' Birth

The people needed to maintain their identity. The exiled nations, torn from their motherland, held on to their customs and traditions that were the strongest elements of their culture in order to maintain their identity. Generally, they struggled to preserve their language and religion, along with those things that had been a part of their lives since childhood.

Israel had already returned from the exile some centuries before, but now it was enslaved under the political and military power of Rome. Their oppressors attempted to impose on them their Greco-Roman culture, but with little success. The Israelites demonstrated their nationalistic tenacity by maintaining their religion and all the traditions that had been created through it. They even had a Jewish governor, Herod the Great (we'll see later how Herod came to be Jewish).

Herod knew that the best way to maintain national unity and the identity of his people was through religion, so he decided to begin rebuilding the temple in Jerusalem. This doesn't mean that he was an exceptional patriot who wanted the best for his people. In fact, he was one of the most ruthless, cruel governors the Hebrew people ever had, but in his ambition, he recognized that a united people is easier to govern.

The Gospel writer Mark records how the disciples admired the majesty of the temple:

> Look, Teacher! What massive stones! What magnificent buildings! (Mark 13:1)

They were all so proud of this great building! Imagine the joy of the Jews who went to Jerusalem once a year from every corner of Palestine and from the other foreign countries where they lived. From a distance they could see the "Holy City," and on the highest hill, the temple, their place of meeting, the center of the presence of God. Anyone who dared to speak ill of the temple was punished.

The temple was venerated to such a degree that those who lived in Jerusalem succeeded in getting the government to exempt them from certain taxes simply because they lived in the "Holy City" where the "Holy Temple" was. They cared for, protected, and maintained the temple so that the rest of the Hebrews could maintain their identity and religion. The people who lived in the country were jealous of this privilege enjoyed by those living in the capital, to the point that it provoked a constant tension between them.

Besides the economic injustices that were generated through the temple, there were such uprisings in the countryside that the peace of the city was disrupted. The subversives repeatedly advanced toward Jerusalem during a festival in order to take some important person captive as a political prisoner. Remember the words of the chief priests, the scribes, and the elders of the people when they met in the courtyard of the high priest, plotting a way to trap Jesus; they said:

> But not during the Feast . . . or there may be a riot among the people. (Matthew 26:5)

They knew very well that political and social riots ended up in uproars in the temple.

On the other hand, there were thousands of people who lived off the temple. Many were employed finishing the work, and many others benefited economically every day from the sales of all that was used for worship and sacrifices. How could anyone dare to speak against the temple?

> Do you see all these great buildings? . . . Not one stone here will be left on another; every one will be thrown down. (Mark 13:2)

How must these words of Jesus have sounded in the ears of those who lived off the temple and who often considered it to be more holy than God Himself? Surely there were those besides the disciples who heard this prophecy and anything else Jesus said in relation to the temple, and used His words against Him during His trial before the Council (Mark 14:58).

But beyond the political and social differences between the people in Jesus' times, the Gospels point to a basic distinction among the people of Israel. On one side were the common people, the needy, those who rejoiced at the coming of the Savior and followed Him everywhere to receive a blessing from His hand. Matthew writes:

> Jesus went through all the towns and villages, teaching . . . , preaching . . . and healing every disease and sickness. When He saw the crowds, He had compassion on them, because they were harassed and helpless, like sheep without a shepherd. (Matthew 9:35–36)

There were not just two or three who were "harassed and helpless." There were multitudes. It wasn't strange, then, that these helpless crowds looked for and followed Jesus. There were moments in which Jesus was crushed in a crowd of people trying to reach Him to be touched by His hand or to touch His cloak and be healed (Matthew 9:20–21; 14:34–36). At other times, Jesus wanted to leave the crowd and sail on a boat across the lake, but the people would run along the shore to wait for Him on the other side (Mark 6:30–33). Sometimes the adults would bring their children to Jesus to the point of irritating the disciples so that they would deny them access (Matthew 19:13).

This group of helpless and needy people were not all Hebrews. It is significant that Jesus praised the faith of a Canaanite woman (Matthew 15:21–28), and that He marveled at the faith of a Roman centurion whose servant was gravely tormented. Jesus says:

> I tell you the truth, I have not found anyone in Israel with such great faith. (Matthew 8:10)

Jesus is not stopped by social or ethnic boundaries, and He doesn't discriminate among the needy.

It is very interesting to see how Jesus, practically speaking, would divide the society of His day into classes: "righteous" and "sinners," or "the healthy" and "the sick" (Matthew 9:12–13).

The "healthy" and the "righteous" are represented by the religious leaders, the Sadducees, the scribes, and the Pharisees, who were tied more to their traditions and their own interpretations of the Law than to Scripture itself. Jesus warned His disciples to be careful with the "yeast" (teaching) of the Pharisees (Matthew 16:6). The "healthy" and the "righteous" are those who came close to Jesus, not to learn from Him, but to tempt Him or to demand He perform some miracle to convince them of His divine authority (Matthew 16:1). Jesus was not moved to feel compassion for them, but rather to distance Himself from them and leave them immersed in their own self-righteousness (Matthew 16:4).

Read Luke 18:9–14.

Reflect on the basic distinction that Jesus makes between the people in this parable.

Read Matthew 15:1–14, 21–28.

Compare the attitude of the Canaanite woman with the attitude of the Pharisees toward Jesus.

Part 3:
The Righteous or the Sinners: Where Do I Fit?

I'm an immigrant in the land of testing. Some years ago, I moved with my family in search of new horizons. I would have to say that I followed God's call to leave the land of my fathers to seek adventure in a new world, but I don't dare. Although at times it's difficult for me to recognize the call of God, I do recognize that the Lord granted me, through this immigration, a new place to carry out my mission in life.

I am not the only immigrant in my family. My ancestors migrated from Western to Eastern Europe and remained there for a generation or so, preserving their language, their customs, and their religion. Both my maternal and my paternal grandparents immigrated from Eastern Europe to South America, taking with them that same language, customs, and religion. I have only a few photos of my grandparents, and I don't have any information about their way of life, but it is significant that the information I could learn from a church publication and from my father's recollection had to do with their Christian faith. I know the day they were born, when they were baptized, when they married, who the pastor was, and what Bible passages were used at their wedding ceremony. Everything else is of little importance. I give thanks to God for this family legacy. I believe it's a testimony of what was really important to them, and I hope that testimony will encourage my family and me, now that we are also immigrants, to preserve our language, our customs, and our religion.

I don't know if every generation in my family understood that God would take them to the land of testing. Usually, immigrants are escaping from situations of poverty or war and are searching for a peaceful place that affords more safety and economic stability. We are not interested in being citizens of the land of testing, but of the land of promise, where we can live out our dreams and desires.

But I'm beginning to realize that God takes care of things in a different way. I believe that any country in this world can be considered the land of testing, and migrations can be seen as opportunities that God gives us to testify of His passion for humankind.

No country in the world is a spiritual "Promised Land." Rather, every place on this planet is a land occupied by two kinds of people: those who consider themselves to be righteous and healthy, and those who anxiously look for a word of comfort and strength. Both desperately need a Savior.

I've met people so proud of their religious tradition that they scorn the newly converted or those who don't understand or live the Christian faith in the same way they do. They lock themselves into rituals and forms so that they can't conceive that God can be recognized, experienced, or worshiped in any way other than their own. They are the Pharisees of our times who believe that they know everything and criticize openly or privately anyone who doesn't follow the same traditions of their ancestors.

Sometimes I find myself among them. I like traditions. I like to belong to a select group that has "access to the temple" because I'm a man and a clergyman. I have a Christian tradition that goes back several generations. I've realized that I look with scorn on those who don't believe as I do. I can't seem to understand how there are people who would rather worship saints and the Virgin instead of following the clear teachings of the Bible. I don't have the patience to testify to them. Criticizing them is much easier. Sometimes I even come to Jesus to tempt Him, that He might give me a clear sign that He has everything under control—as if the promise found in His Word isn't enough for me. I demand, I criticize, I justify myself, setting myself apart from the rest and placing myself among the selected ones who are just like me.

When I realize what a Pharisee I am, I feel ashamed. I look around me and find that there are poor widows who give a greater offering than mine, because they give everything they have. I look a little farther and I see recent converts, full of the joy of the Holy Spirit, who can't stop talking about what God has done in their lives. I ask God to touch my heart once again and make me sensitive to His love and His calling.

There are times when I feel very anxious and needy, traveling across the lakeshore of my days, searching for Jesus. Thank God, I always find Him, and when I do and spend time with Him, I ask myself how I could make it through a single day without feeling His presence. This is the reason I go to Holy Communion every Sunday, because I don't want to miss the opportunity to be with Him. There, I can stretch out my hand to touch Him and experience His healing. I brought my children into His presence so they could be reborn in Baptism and begin to live out their Christian calling.

I understand that I'm not alone in this situation. I'm just one of a great multitude constantly looking for reassurance, peace, comfort, and eternal security. Now, since I have been redeemed by Jesus, my search is over, because His promise to be with me through eternity is a reality. But I don't underestimate the power of evil, that Pharisee that appears in me at every opportunity, those doubts that make me question the ways of the Lord and tempt Him by asking for special signs in my life. No, the search for reassurance of God's love in a dangerous world, in this land of testing, never ends. It is not so bad because Jesus is always among us in His Word and Sacraments, accompanying us on our migrations, helping us testify to our faith and the reason for our joy in a world that is at once Pharisaic in its judgment and profoundly in need of health and peace.

I also realize that my encounters with Jesus don't depend on me, because I don't always seek Him as I should or need to. It does me good to know that He looks for me first; He comes to the lakeshore of my life to find me. He seeks me out in order to tend to my needs, to call me, and to send me, time and time again. I love to see Him coming with His tender face and outstretched arms to surround me with His love and compassion.

Read Luke 11:53–54.

Describe the attitude of the scribes and Pharisees, and think about similar attitudes that you might have toward Jesus.

Read Mark 6:30–34.

Reflect on the needs of the crowd that followed Jesus. Think about your own needs and how Jesus shows His compassion to you.

Chapter 3

Part 1: *The Birth of Jesus*

(Matthew 1:18–25; Luke 2:1–20)

Each stage of Jesus' life was extraordinary, and His birth was no exception. When the angel told Mary that she was going to have a baby, she was living in northern Palestine, in a small town called Nazareth. From there, Mary made two journeys of momentous importance. The first was to a town in the mountains of Judea to visit her aged cousin Elizabeth, who was also pregnant by God's design. Those first three months of her pregnancy, Mary stayed with Elizabeth. How many conversations about their future children must they have had? How many dreams and fears must they have shared? John, later called "the Baptist," and Jesus shared the same roof, although it was before they were born.

The apostle Paul says:

> But when the time had fully come, God sent His Son, born of a woman. (Galatians 4:4)

The fulfillment of time means the moment God had prepared and coordinated with much care. On one hand, the heavens were mobilized. First was the angel Gabriel, who visited Zechariah, John's father, and later, Mary. Then an angel visited Joseph in his dreams and guided him through all that would happen. Later on, a multitude of angels appeared outside Bethlehem to announce the birth of Jesus.

On the other hand, God was also coordinating the activity on earth. It wasn't an accident that Caesar Augustus gave the edict to begin a census in the entire Roman Empire, thus causing Joseph and Mary to go to Bethlehem, where, according to the prophecies, the Messiah would be born (Matthew 2:6). This was Mary's second momentous journey.

The other prophecy that would be fulfilled made the birth of Jesus the most extraordinary event in the history of humankind:

> All this took place to fulfill what the Lord had said through the prophet: "The virgin will be with child and will give birth to a son, and they will call Him Immanuel"—which means, "God with us." (Matthew 1:22–23)

Jesus' virginal birth was extraordinary because it required the special intervention of the Holy Spirit; but above all, it was because of the way God chose to be "with us." God, an infinite and inaccessible spirit, became a human being, simple, tender, fragile, and vulnerable. God chose to be "with us" and to be like us in order to experience suffering, anxiety, temptation of the devil, and even death, in His own flesh. God chose to be "with us" in order to feel what we feel and to express His love for us in a way we can understand.

And the extraordinary continues to happen. Again, the heavens entered into the activity, showing the star that God had saved just for this occasion. It appeared far from Bethlehem, in the East, the edge of the Promised Land. What a contradiction! Something great happens near Jerusalem, and no one knows about it. The news that the King of the Jews had been born arrived at Jerusalem from far away, from an eastern country, by means of people who were not Jews. It's paradoxical, because if you go to Bethlehem today, you will see the radio and television towers of Jerusalem, and you can go by car from one city to the other in only twenty minutes.

It is interesting to see how God's plan works. Approximately seven centuries earlier, the people of Israel had been taken captive to the eastern countries. They stayed there many years until they were permitted to return to Palestine. During the captivity, evidently some Jews were very effective in their testimony and shared their faith and the Holy Scriptures with the people around them, because several centuries later, a group of astronomers saw a new star in the heavens and possibly associated it with Balaam's prophecy:

> A star will come out of Jacob; a scepter will rise out of Israel. (Numbers 24:17)

And they saw the star that curiously took them through Jerusalem before arriving in Bethlehem.

It is notable that the strangers who had received the testimony of God's Word from the Hebrew people didn't sit around waiting for something to happen. They investigated and searched for signs, and when they saw them, they would know exactly what was happening.

Herod and the people of Jerusalem, near Bethlehem, knew nothing. Although there were experts in Jerusalem

(Matthew 2:3–6), they didn't react as the Wise Men did. They didn't understand the signs of the times—or even *see* them. Worse yet, Herod, some time afterward, seeing he had been tricked, ordered that all baby boys in Bethlehem and the surrounding area be killed in order to eliminate possible competition for his throne. The attitude of the foreign Wise Men was better than that of the king of the Jews.

Scripture does not say how many Wise Men arrived in Jerusalem. Tradition always speaks of three because there were three gifts brought to Jesus: gold, incense, and myrrh. However, three people never traveled alone in the desert, especially if they were carrying such precious gifts. History testifies that in those days, caravans were never fewer than fifty camels—and some reached as many as one thousand—as a way of mutual support and protection. There were certainly more than three foreigners who upset King Herod and all of Jerusalem.

When the Wise Men arrived from the East to worship Jesus in Bethlehem and to present their treasures to Him, Isaiah's prophecy was fulfilled:

> To you the riches of the nations will come. (Isaiah 60:5)

The riches that God has prepared for us for the expansion of His kingdom are not found only in the "Promised Land." God has "gifts," people, and material goods in the least likely places. God prepared those gifts over centuries so that they might be ready for His Son at the time of His birth. God plans and coordinates—and takes His time.

Read Matthew 1:18–2:12 and Luke 2:1–20.

Count how many uncommon or extraordinary things happened in the story of the birth of Jesus.

Read 2 Kings 5.

Think about how God's message was spoken in the Gentile countries.

Part 2:
The Presentation of Jesus in the Temple
(Luke 2:21–38)

The Flight to Egypt
(Matthew 2:13–15)

Just a little over a week after Jesus' birth, He received His name and was circumcised. His parents thus fulfilled the requirements of the Law. There were no exceptions or privileges for the Son of the Most High and the future King of the world. It was clear that God had sent His Son into the world:

> God sent His Son, born of a woman, born under law. (Galatians 4:4)

About a month later, Mary and Joseph, as faithful believers, went to fulfill another requirement established by the Law: the presentation their child to the Lord. Little did they imagine what surprises were in store for them. Their experience in the temple was to be much richer than they had ever thought possible. It would surpass any other sacrifice of purification.

While Mary, Joseph, and Jesus were traveling to Jerusalem, the Holy Spirit had moved a righteous and pious elderly man so he would encounter them at the temple. Simeon surely had the most fascinating experience of his long life when the Holy Spirit revealed to him that he would see the Anointed One of God before he died. What more could a pious man who trusted in God hope for than the consolation of God for His people? (Luke

2:25). His heart started racing when he saw Mary and Joseph with the Lord's Anointed. He extended his hands, and his arms were made strong to hold God who came to be "with us." From his mouth flowed the eloquent words that clearly expressed the mission of the Messiah. Simeon might have summarized God's action: "I can die in peace now because I see the promise of God; I'm holding it in my hands. I see in Him salvation not only for me, but for all the people of all the ethnic groups of the world."

For centuries, the Christian Church has used Simeon's words at the end of the liturgy of public worship, because it recognized in them the best way to end a worship service. The participants have heard the proclamation of salvation in the preaching of the Word; they have seen and been with Jesus in Holy Communion; and now they can go in peace to share the light of the world with others.

Simeon continues, now blessing the parents and announcing to Mary what would happen in days to come. Simeon intended to prepare Mary for the times of suffering that lay ahead, but they are not easy words to accept. We cannot possibly imagine or feel the pain of a mother seeing her son beaten and hung on a cross to die like a criminal. Mary would have time from this moment on to work through these concepts in her heart and mind. She would need to understand them in the context surrounding Jesus as He would carry out His ministry. Many would follow her Son, but many more would reject Him. God, in His loving care, was warning Mary beforehand of what her motherhood would cost her.

At the same time, another elderly person appeared, a woman of good reputation, who lived out her ministry by fasting and praying every day in the temple. Anna spoke convincingly of the redemption God was offering to those who hoped in Him. Mary and Joseph listened attentively, thinking and treasuring in their hearts all the testimonies they experienced that day. They would need this to face the future.

And the future did not make them wait. After the Wise Men returned to their own country, Joseph was warned again by an angel: Jesus' life was in danger. Poor Joseph! Since becoming engaged to Mary, he had not stopped having dreams that changed his life moment by moment. Now that the visitors had gone, he thought that things might calm down a little. He and Mary could plan their return to Nazareth, or make other plans for the future. He never thought his Son would receive a death threat! He might have expected an illness, or a little fever, or that He might be a victim of an epidemic. But a death threat! Joseph understood that there was no time to lose. He took the Child and His mother and left the country.

The story that follows in the Gospel of Matthew after the flight to Egypt is one of the cruelest incidents recorded in the New Testament. Herod shows his brutality. Before this, he had commanded that his own wife, Mariamne, be killed, and three of his sons, and many from outside his family, because he suspected that they would rob him of his throne. Herod's greatest problem was that he was not a Jew by birth but by conversion. He was the son of an Edomite father and a Nabatean mother, and although his family had been in Judea for many generations, he was never accepted by the Hebrew people as a true Jew. This explains why Herod was so disturbed when the Wise Men from the East asked him:

> Where is the one who has been born king of the Jews? (Matthew 2:2)

A Jewish-born king had a greater chance of being accepted and loved by the people than an adopted Jew.

Herod was not going to risk his throne, so he launched a massacre of innocent children.

The devil, God's number one enemy, had closely followed the plan of salvation from the moment God promised Adam and Eve that He would send a Savior to rescue the world. The devil was attentive and tortured and commanded the killing of the prophets and other servants of the Lord each time he thought the plan for salvation was advancing. When Jesus was born, the tempter unleashed all his fury to annihilate every possibility that the King of the Jews might stay alive. His plan was comprehensive, encompassing all boys under the age of two from Bethlehem and its surroundings. The soldiers, under Herod's command, had no pity. Without the least consideration, they spread terror and pain in many families. The cost of the world's salvation was just beginning to be felt.

Read Luke 2:21–28.

Think about the blessing of Simeon and the ministry of Anna.

Read Matthew 2:13–18 and Jeremiah 31:15.

Reflect on the cost that some families paid, losing their children in King Herod's brutal attack.

Reflect on the brutality of the devil's attempt to interfere with God's plan for salvation.

Part 3:
I Hope I Get to Be an Old Man

I believe the biggest mistake I've made in my life was to underestimate the power of evil. I never thought evil could be so bad. It seems that for a long period of my life, I lived in a bubble that sheltered me from the atrocities of the devil. I've been a Christian since I was baptized, just a few days old. I grew up in a Christian family, and all my life, I've been involved with the work of the Church. I had little contact with the "real world" that didn't share the Law of God or His mercy. But one day it struck me. Evil destroyed my innocence and provoked a sharp, infuriating pain. I lived experiences that opened my eyes to the power of evil and helped me not to underestimate the power of the devil and, at the same time, to understand the immensity of God's love. Now I understand better the petition Jesus taught me in the Lord's Prayer:

> Deliver us from the evil one. (Matthew 6:13)

I can't imagine the parents' pain at the loss of their children in Bethlehem at Herod's hands. I can't imagine the cold chill that ran through Mary when she heard Simeon's words:

> And a sword will pierce your own soul too. (Luke 2:35)

Nor can I imagine the anxiety of Joseph's family when they got up one day and found that Jesus and His parents were not there anymore.

The opportunities to experience the power of evil in life seem to be around every corner, while the opportunities to feel blessing and joy are hidden. They come to me in the words of Jesus:

> In this world you will have trouble. But take heart! I have overcome the world. (John 16:33)

And they come to me in His words to Simon Peter:

> Simon, Simon, Satan has asked to sift you as wheat. But I have prayed for you, Simon, that your faith may not fail. (Luke 22:31–32)

It's clear. I can't say Jesus didn't warn me. I really admire His appreciation of reality. I should recognize that He never said my life would be easy. I like the words of the preacher who said:

> Jesus doesn't make our life easier, but He makes it glorious.

His own life wasn't easy, but it was absolutely glorious. I would like to have as honest an appreciation for reality as Jesus had.

At times, I'm delighted by the angels, with all the host of heaven that God has ready to care for me and direct me. I admire the gold, incense, and myrrh He brings out from who knows where, so that we, His children, lack nothing. Many times, I only have eyes to see His gifts, His care, His meticulous planning for my life. Sometimes I think about the millions of angels that are waiting for me at the moment of my death with their brightness, their smiles, and their warmth. Surely that was the welcome that Simeon and Anna had when God called them to His glory.

One time, during Lent, I went to a worship service that was celebrated at noon and attended by many elderly members of the congregation. The majority of them walked with a cane, or supported on someone's arm.

They reminded me of Simeon and Anna, because they, too, were there, in the temple, worshiping and singing as they were able, sure that God, who came to be "with us," was their strength and support. I remember that worship service intensely. I received from those elderly people a powerful testimony of faith for my life. That day, I had one more proof of the way God testifies to me of His love and faithfulness, of how He provides people and occasions to encourage me to keep moving forward in life.

And now I am an exile, somewhat voluntarily. I had to learn another language. There is a hole in my heart for my family that is so far away. Now that I think about it, I don't know where so many gifts came from that helped us establish ourselves in a new country. Somehow God provided everything we needed. No, I'm not comparing myself to Jesus; only it seems fascinating that He went through so many of the same things we go through, and I remember the words of the New Testament:

> He had to be made like His brothers in every way. (Hebrews 2:17)

This helps me understand His name even better, *Immanuel*, "God with us."

Herod's brutality makes me think of those devastating, diabolical attacks I see around me that attempt to keep God from doing His good work with humankind: the killings in our schools; the thousands of innocent children who are killed at the hands of abortionists before they're even born; the lack of respect for the life God creates with such loving care; the people who die slowly, poisoned by drugs. The devil respects neither age nor authority. He tramples on everything and leaves a pool of blood. Sometimes it seems that Jesus is far away, fleeing from all this, fleeing to Egypt to save His life. But when I really think about it, I know He only went away for a time in order to be able to make Himself greater and to face my salvation and the salvation of the whole world with all available strength, to triumph once and for all over the root of evil and all its destructive powers of evil.

The Wise Men had to return to their own country by another route, going well out of their way in order to avoid passing through Jerusalem. This was a trial because they already knew the way, but they had to venture out in another direction. Mary and Joseph had to go to Egypt instead of staying in Bethlehem or returning to Nazareth. Simeon and Anna had to wait until almost the end of their days to live their richest experiences. Surely the waiting wasn't important to them, as returning to their home by another route was not important to the Wise Men.

Several times, God has also made me go by another way. I can't always go directly where I want to go, and I can't go back the way I came because God has other plans. It's hard for me to accept it at first because I don't see as God sees. I don't understand His way of working. But I need to learn to trust Him because perhaps I might have the blessing Simeon and Anna had, that God might use me until the very end of my days to proclaim His Good News as they did, with energy and boldness.

Read Matthew 2:19–23.

Think about the outstanding points of this passage.

Analyze the attitude of care that God had for Jesus from His earliest infancy.

Read Isaiah 60:1–6.

Find points in common with Matthew 2:1–12.

What does it mean to you that God so perfectly fulfilled the prophecies?

Chapter 4

Part 1:
John and Jesus

(Matthew 3)

Sara and Joshua have been married for many years. They live in a small community on the outskirts of Galilee, and while they take a break from their daily chores, Sara decides to share something with her husband that's been bothering her for months.

Sara: Will you come with me? Most of our neighbors have gone already. The whole world is talking about him. I'm curious about this preacher.

Joshua: What could be so special about him? I heard he goes around with long hair and only has one change of clothes. He can't be very clean.

Sara: I don't believe you can tell what kind of person he is just by his appearance. You have to listen to what he says. They say he's a really good speaker and has had quite a lot to say to the Pharisees and the teachers of the Law.

Joshua: Yes, but it will take us all day to get to the Jordan River.

Sara: Don't you think it's worth the effort, spending a day on the road, to listen to a prophet? There hasn't been a prophet among us for years. Maybe he really could be sent by God. Remember that his birth was a little unusual because his parents were really old when he was born.

Joshua: And you, what sins do *you* have to confess? It seems like that's what the people are going to him for. Besides, he baptizes people. Do you want to be baptized too and join some elite group?

Sara: I don't know if I want to belong to a special group, but it wouldn't do me any harm to confess my sins and be baptized.

Joshua: I would like to know what sins people are confessing! I'd go just to hear that!

This couple from Galilee decides to make the journey to the Jordan River to see the renowned preacher who was becoming more famous every day, the one people called "the Baptist." They don't imagine that they are going to be present at one of the most notable moments in history. During the trip, they have long conversations about their marriage and the sadness that overcomes them every time they remember that they haven't been able to have children. Maybe this is why they're going to see the Baptist; they heard he was born in his parents' old age. Waiting is hard . . . waiting and waiting without any sure sign that what they are waiting for would ever happen. Waiting, as the whole nation of Israel was waiting, for some sign that God would indeed finally send the Messiah. It had been four centuries since they had received any revelation from God. Could it be that this Baptist is the most important sign to come before the coming of the Messiah? The Baptist is saying incredible things:

> The ax is already at the root of the trees, and every tree that does not produce good fruit will be cut down and thrown into the fire. (Matthew 3:10)

We had better take him seriously!

Joshua: They say that the Baptist is announcing the coming of Someone even more powerful than him. They talk of a baptism with fire and spirit. I've never heard of such a thing. What could all this mean?

Sara: I don't know, but maybe we'll find out soon. Something big must be happening, because people are coming from all over, even from Jerusalem, to listen to him and to be baptized.

John the Baptist is preaching exuberantly when he sees his cousin coming. He already knows about Him and His irreproachable conduct. He remembers well what his cousin's mother, Mary, told about the time when Jesus left the doctors of the Law in the temple amazed at His understanding—when He was just twelve years old! What will happen here? He doesn't need to be baptized. What sins could He possibly have to confess? None! How could His life be any more perfect? "I might use this chance to be baptized by Him," John must have thought. He didn't just think it; he said it directly:

> I need to be baptized by You, and do You come to me? (Matthew 3:14)

What a paradox! John, a sinner like the rest of us, baptizes Jesus, the holiest of all holy people who ever walked the earth. John baptizes the One who has no need to repent and who needs no forgiveness of sins. It is possible that John may not have understood, but he obeyed, and this makes John the most major prophet of all times. His mission was to prepare the people for the coming of Jesus by touching their consciences and by denouncing the oppression caused by those in power, the moral corruption of the authorities, and the abuse inflicted by the military. John called attention to the religious leaders who turned the people away from true religion. Jesus did the same. John ended up beheaded; Jesus hung on a cross. Proclaiming God's truth to a sinful society has its risks. Jesus knew this, and for this reason, He asked John to baptize Him. He needed to be publicly anointed as the Father had planned. Jesus wanted that couple from Galilee, John, and everyone there to be able to recognize Him as the One sent from the Father.

Jesus came to be with us. He is Immanuel. But it wasn't easy for Him to be with us. The power of sin was manifested everywhere: in the arrogance of the powerful, in illnesses, in infertility, in spiritual darkness. Jesus wants to accomplish "all righteousness," beginning His ministry with the backing of God the Father in heaven and with the power of the Holy Spirit. There is no other way. It takes all the power of God to defeat the darkness that surrounds human life. The triune God was present in Jesus' Baptism, manifesting His good will toward His creation.

Sara: Did you see what just happened? I've never experienced anything like it! I've never breathed air so light or seen such a great light and splendor on the Jordan River. I could hardly believe what I was seeing!

Joshua: You'd better believe it, because I saw the same thing. Come on! I want to get a closer look at the One who takes away the sins of the world. Maybe He'll have a word of encouragement for us.

The couple from Galilee weren't disappointed. No one who recognizes Jesus as the Lamb of God who takes away the sin of the world feels disappointed. It had been well worth the trouble to leave the day's work and go to see the Baptist. In the end, they had found themselves with Immanuel, with God Himself, who Himself was baptized "to fulfill all righteousness" (Matthew 3:15) and so to be with them forever. They would never forget this experience. Neither would John the Baptist.

Later on, when his fearless denunciation of King Herod got him thrown in jail, John thought long and hard about Jesus' ministry and sent his followers to ask:

> Are You the one who was to come, or should we expect someone else? (Matthew 11:3)

He didn't have to wait long for Jesus' answer:

> The blind receive sight, the lame walk, those who have leprosy are cured, the deaf hear, the dead are raised, and the good news is preached to the poor. (Matthew 11:5)

Only a loving and deeply compassionate God could have made such changes in people's lives. John must have been well satisfied with this answer.

Read John 1:19–34.

Find three outstanding aspects of John's preaching.

How do those aspects compare with preaching heard today?

Read Isaiah 4:1–11.

Think about the description of preaching that Isaiah predicts about John the Baptist.

In what sense did John the Baptist prepare the way for Jesus' ministry?

Part 2:
The Devil Returns to Attack: The Temptation
(Matthew 4:1–11)

A preacher friend of mine used to say that people love to hear about the devil. There must be something morbid—or perhaps a mysterious air—about the devil. What is the devil like? A serpent? Does he really exist? I believe that these days, many societies have not only denied the existence of God, but also the existence of the devil. You hear something about the devil, or "the tempter," as it says in Matthew 4, but very little. He seems antiquated, almost a myth, and since the devil was never made flesh as God was made flesh in Jesus, he's hard to identify.

The apostle Paul was always aware of his presence and described him as the principal enemy of believers. This is what he writes to the members of the Christian congregation in Ephesus:

> Put on the full armor of God so that you can take your stand against the devil's schemes. For our struggle is not against flesh and blood, but against the rulers, against the authorities, against the powers of this dark world and against the spiritual forces of evil in the heavenly realms. (Ephesians 6:11–12)

It was those rulers of darkness that moved the heart of Herod to kill in cold blood the baby boys of Bethlehem after Jesus was born. Now those rulers of darkness came back to attack Jesus. The Baptism was over. Jesus was anointed with the Holy Spirit to begin His public ministry of reconciliation, and now He goes to the desert. He needs to be alone to meditate on His future ministry, and to strengthen His spirit to develop His vocation with all His might.

Did He really have to spend forty days in solitude and fasting? Without a doubt. The Gospels say that the disciples tried to cast out an evil spirit from a boy, but they couldn't do it. When Jesus later cast out that spirit, they asked:

> "Why couldn't we drive it out?" [Jesus] replied, "This kind can come out only by prayer." (Mark 9:28–29)

Jesus knew all too well whom He was facing. That is why He followed the Holy Spirit to the desert and spent forty days fasting, meditating, and preparing Himself through prayer for the work of saving mankind.

And the devil, as always, was lying in wait, ready to ambush Him. He waited until Jesus was hungry. He waited until Jesus was just ready to return to His people, to enjoy a good bath, eat freshly baked bread, be with His family, and sleep in a real bed. He waited long enough to find Jesus at His weakest possible moment. But he was mistaken. The tempter didn't know that in Jesus' mind, His Father's words, spoken from heaven forty days earlier, still resonated:

> This is My Son, whom I love; with Him I am well pleased. (Matthew 3:17)

The tempter thought he could make Jesus doubt that He was the Son of God, so he challenged Him to use His divine power to provide food for Himself.

It didn't seem like a big temptation, really. What could Jesus have to lose by turning stones into bread? But it's

Jesus' attitude we need to observe. He didn't discuss the matter with the devil. He didn't need to convince the devil of anything. That was not His work. He didn't come to the world to match forces with the powers of evil, but to defeat them once and for all. Jesus didn't waste time trying to convince the devil He was the Son of God. He simply responded with words from Scripture:

> Man does not live on bread alone, but on every word that comes from the mouth of God. (Matthew 4:4)

The second temptation doesn't seem to make sense. Trying to prove what the Bible says is true? Defy nature's laws only to show the devil who rules over more? Perhaps the devil underestimated Jesus and hoped that He would hurl Himself into the air and be dashed to pieces on the rocks below. Only someone desperate would come up with such an idea. And without a doubt, the devil was desperate. He could see his imminent defeat coming closer.

The devil wanted to stop Jesus at any cost, and now went to the lengths of offering Jesus more than a simple challenge. He offered Him all the kingdoms of the earth!

This temptation was a bit more substantial. Perhaps with this, the tempter could successfully distract Jesus from His ministry. The devil offered what he didn't have. Jesus knew very well that the devil didn't own the world and had not the least authority to offer it to Jesus. In any case, Satan only reigns over the forces of evil, something in which Jesus has no interest. In the end, what interested Jesus was the total destruction of those kingdoms of darkness.

Jesus continues without entering into a dialogue with the devil. He only answers with words from Scripture and does not give place to any conversation or negotiation.

He doesn't play with Satan. God's own Son does not underestimate the power of evil. He doesn't do as Eve did in the Garden of Eden, entering into conversation with the devil. He simply casts him out of His presence.

Two things demand profound attention in this temptation experience. First, the devil knows the Scriptures, but in his cunning and malice, he cites them out of context and with the intent to cause harm. The devil uses Scripture in a twisted way to challenge what God says through them. That wasn't the reason why God gave His Word to His people. Second, Jesus also knows the Scriptures, and He cites them so well that He is able to drive the devil away.

The Gospel of Luke ends the temptation story, saying:

> When the devil had finished all this tempting,
> he left Him until an opportune time. (Luke 4:13)

Jesus' triumph before temptation was only temporary. The devil hadn't been beaten; he only went away . . . for a time. Time and time again, the devil came back during Jesus' ministry. He would use Peter to try to distract Him from His mission. He would use His own brothers to try to turn Him aside from His salvation work. He tried everything, and he tried with all his might, but in the end, he was beaten.

Nothing to eat for forty days, and having to withstand such temptation! But God was attentive. He sent His angels to be with His dearly beloved Son and to serve Him. God was closely watching the progress of His Son in the work of saving mankind.

Read Ephesians 6:10–17.

Think about the elements Paul gives us Christians to withstand the attacks of the devil.

Part 3:
What Is My Desert?

I wish I could be John the Baptist. I'm impressed by his eloquence, but above all, by his bravery. He never minced words. He wasn't intimidated by the religious leaders or by King Herod. Of course, I wouldn't like to be John the Baptist at the moment he was thrown into jail, much less when they cut off his head. I think I would like to be like him just to cleanse people of their sins. It would be a way for me to satisfy my desire to be better than everyone else. I realize that. I understand that the couple from Galilee went to see John the Baptist just to see what kind of sins people would confess. There's something morbid inside me that leads me to point out the sins of others.

I must recognize that I am far from being like John the Baptist, especially when I observe that he denounced sins only to show the need we all have to be reconciled to God. For this very reason, the main purpose behind his preaching was to point to Jesus as the Lamb of God who takes away the sin of the world. His preaching was so clear that his own disciples left him to follow Jesus (John 1:35–40). What an example of a preacher!

It's interesting to see how carefully God prepared for Jesus to come on the scene. He didn't surprise the people by striking the world with a startling blow. On the contrary, He began to make people aware, through the Baptist, of their situation. Very precisely, He pointed out the sins of the authorities, soldiers, religious leaders, and the people in general. It's as if people's consciences were asleep and had to be awakened.

I often need a John the Baptist to show me where I stand, because I still would rather look at others than myself. Sometimes I realize how I try to avoid my own faults. It's a good thing the Baptist continues preaching yet today through God's Word. He still keeps on presenting Jesus with incredible clarity as the Lamb of God who takes away the sin of the world.

It sometimes seems that I need to spend more time in the desert. John's preaching and Jesus' Baptism and temptation occurred in desert places. Certain things need a special place, and I think about my desert, that place where I can go and recognize my need for a Savior. I don't doubt that one of those places, possibly my most excellent "Jordan," is the church where I meet weekly with others to publicly confess my sins and then listen to the words of absolution. The Lamb of God is always there, renewing me and giving me peace. But then I leave that place only to find myself in another desert full of dangers and temptations.

That's how I see the world some days, a place full of dangers and temptations—but mostly temptations. I don't see the devil, but I see diabolical structures in society that denigrate God's creation. I see organized crime, collective and individual sins, wars, gangs, swindles, frauds, pornography, and death. Every day we see more examples of how the rulers of darkness wreak havoc in the world.

But the devil doesn't have to be bloody or violent. He also does his work in very subtle ways, planting seeds of doubt. The Gospel writer Matthew calls him "tempter" because that is his work. One of the most impressive things about the devil's temptation of Jesus is how he tries to make Jesus doubt that He is the Son of God. The first two times, the devil approaches Jesus, saying:

> If You are the Son of God, tell these stones to become bread. (Matthew 4:3)

It seems unrealDone that the devil should be so determined to sow seeds of doubt about what the Father had said so clearly from heaven a few days before:

> This is My Son, whom I love; with Him I am well pleased. (Matthew 3:17)

This makes me think of all the times I have doubted who I am. In spite of God's constant reassurance that I am His child, sometimes I feel unworthy of considering myself as such. These are the times when the devil takes advantage, reaffirming those doubts of mine: "Of *course* you don't deserve to be God's child with all the things you do!"

Other times, I hear him saying, "Don't think God will forgive that sin so easily. You'll have to work hard to make Him forget it!"

The rulers of darkness are insistent and try to make me doubt that God has given me any gifts. They constantly say, "You won't be able to do it. It's too much for you. You're not fit for this work. Leave it to someone with more ability than you have."

Through all this, I have to learn from Jesus not to negotiate with the tempter, but to respond with clear words of Scripture so that all the power of evil will depart from me, and to wipe out the doubts that paralyze me and prevent me from living in the freedom to which God called me.

I hope I may have answers as clear as those that Jesus gave so I don't waste time with fruitless arguments or negotiations. I would like to know better how to use the Scriptures since they have a concrete answer for every situation in life.

I know this is an everyday task, because the tempter leaves me only for a little while, waiting for another opportune moment when I'm hungry or suffering some kind of need, or when I feel alone. Every day I need to concentrate on prayer and the Word of God to strengthen my connection with Him.

The apostle Paul serves as an example for me. His attitude toward life and ministry is worth imitating. The same one who said that our struggle is against the powers of this dark world and the spiritual forces of evil in the heavenly realms also affirmed:

> I can do everything through Him who gives me strength. (Philippians 4:13)

These words encourage me, as do the words of the apostle John:

> The one who is in you is greater than the one who is in the world. (1 John 4:4)

Read Matthew 11:2–14.

How does Jesus describe John the Baptist and his ministry?

Read Matthew 12:22–30.

How does Jesus describe His ministry against the devil?

Chapter 5

Part 1:
Jesus Visits His Hometown
(Luke 4:14–30)

Jesus must have been well known and popular because in spite of the fact that in those days there weren't any means of mass communication, Luke the evangelist says that when Jesus returned to Galilee:

> News about Him spread through the whole countryside. (Luke 4:14)

Everybody was speaking about Jesus, and the talk was good.

There was a period of time, approximately eighteen months, in which John the Baptist and Jesus developed their ministries in a parallel manner. Both had disciples, both baptized (John 3:26; 4:2), and both proclaimed the coming of the kingdom of God. During that time, John's mission was to establish Jesus' identity, a task he accomplished with admirable bravery and deep joy (John 3:29). Several times he presented Jesus as:

> The Lamb of God, who takes away the sin of the world! (John 1:29)

John's task was to connect Jesus with the Old Testament lamb that was sacrificed for the forgiveness of sins. The preaching made the common people aware of who Jesus was, and it also alerted the Pharisees and the teachers of the Law, who were surely happy when Herod ordered John thrown in jail. But their happiness was short-lived because once John disappeared from the scene, Jesus came into play even stronger than John. John didn't get jealous when his disciples left him to follow Jesus (John 1:35–37), or when he was put in jail while Jesus remained free. John was an authentic messenger of God and put these words into practice:

> He must become greater; I must become less. (John 3:30)

Jesus was becoming more and more well known everywhere He went. On one occasion, He went back to Nazareth, the little town where He had grown up.

Nazareth was insignificant in several ways. It is never mentioned in the Old Testament and apparently had no historic value. Its geographic location at the top of a hill kept it isolated from the main commercial routes. Nobody passed through Nazareth. In New Testament times, the population was approximately 75 families, some 350 people. There was only one well of water for the entire city, and only one synagogue. Though small and isolated, it wasn't a bad place to raise children. Jesus spent more than twenty years there, so He was well known. This personal knowledge of Jesus had to be put together with His fame that resulted from all His activities in the surrounding areas. Jesus was already admired in Nazareth before His missionary visit. His countrymen and neighbors were proud that someone so famous came from their town. That's why they gave Him the privilege of reading from the Scripture that Sabbath, and not only to read, but to explain its teachings. He was so admired that after Jesus said His first words, they "were amazed at the gracious words that came from His lips" (Luke 4:22).

But that admiration wouldn't last long. The passage from Isaiah that Jesus read was not chosen by chance. It was carefully planned by the Father in heaven so the religious romanticism of the people of Nazareth might be exchanged for a spirituality that would provide solid help for the needy and change the lives of the people who lived in darkness.

Jesus announced in a specific way that God had arrived explicitly to change people's situations. Jesus added a little more and said things that the people would rather not hear. There have always been people who are needy in every sense of the word. There have always been people crying out for a change in their life situation. Jesus mentioned the lepers and widows, two of the neediest sectors of society in those days.

What did God do with these people in Israel in the time of the prophets Elijah and Elisha? Nothing. They were left abandoned because of the unbelief, idolatry, and disobedience that reigned in Israel. Jesus continued by saying that God doesn't stop doing His good work and changing the lives of people, but He does it for other people—for a people who were never a part of the people of Israel, but who were definitely children of God and, as such, the objects of His mercy. In other words, Jesus told them that God's love has no limits. It is not confined within the boundaries of religion. It doesn't stick to just one geographic location, much less accept only one kind of people. Neither the widow from Sidon nor the Syrian leper were part of what the Israelites considered to be the people of God; nevertheless, God showed His compassion to them. With this example, Jesus declared that if His hearers in Nazareth didn't accept God's way of repentance and compassion for others, God would concentrate His attention on other people.

What Jesus was saying was unbearable for the excessively pious people in His own town who believed they were surely protected just because they were descendants of Abraham. They didn't waste any time; they took Jesus from the synagogue and intended to throw Him over the cliff to get rid of Him. Their hometown pride turned to fear and blind hatred. They didn't stop to consider the consequences. They acted on impulse as their hearts directed them, hearts that were closed to the Good News of Jesus.

In a way, the people from Nazareth achieved their purpose of getting rid of Jesus, because He left there and went to carry out His ministry of love among other people.

Was Jesus disappointed because He wasn't accepted by His own neighbors, the ones who had helped Him grow to adulthood? Hardly. It must have hurt Him. But Jesus had no illusions of being accepted or gaining popularity. He came to clearly present God's message for His people. His intention was not to attack anyone. He knew the people of His town and their needs; above all, He knew their powerful need to change their hard hearts, paralyzed by history and traditions, into hearts more sensitive to the needs of others.

Jesus' popularity and the fact that the whole world was speaking well of Him made no difference in Nazareth. Nor did His preaching on the passage of the prophet Isaiah break down the stubbornness of His neighbors. What restraint! Jesus didn't keep insisting they listen to Him. He didn't try to force them to understand what He was saying to them. He just made reference to the plan of God according to the Holy Scriptures. Later on, as a conclusion to some of His teachings, Jesus would say, "He who has ears, let him hear" (Matthew 11:15).

But there were no ears ready to hear God in Nazareth. He had to move on.

Read John 1:35–42.

List the three most important things in this passage that apply to this chapter.

Read Matthew 13:53–58.

Think about Jesus' ministry in Nazareth and its results.

Part 2:
The Gospel Triangle
(Matthew 4:12–17)

At the mouth of the River Jordan, to the north of the Sea of Galilee, three cities lie very close to one another: Capernaum, Korazin, and Bethsaida. Their locations form a triangle. New Testament scholars have named this area the "Gospel Triangle." There is no other place where Jesus did such miracles as He did in this little triangle. To give you an idea of how small this place really is, you can visit all three cities in one day by walking from one to the next. (See Map 4, p. 75.)

Why did Jesus pick such a small area to exercise such an enormous ministry? If the religious center was Jerusalem, why not settle there? Many factors weighed in Jesus' decision to go to the shores of the lake.

Peter and his brother Andrew, two of Jesus' disciples, were originally from Bethsaida, although they also had a house in Capernaum. Jesus made that city His base of operations. Both cities were on the shore of the Sea of Galilee, which, in that day, was considered to be a "gold mine." At the mouth of the Jordan on the north end of the lake were the best fishing grounds. In that same area there were several hot springs, rich in minerals and good for curing and relieving skin diseases, which were very common back then.

Capernaum was also a very important commercial center, where Aramaic and Greek were spoken. Peter's brother Andrew, for example, had a Greek name and served as intermediary so that some Greeks could see Jesus (John 12:20–22). Capernaum, like Bethsaida, was located along the international route that connected Damascus, in Syria, to the Mediterranean Sea. Both Jews and pagans lived there. People from many nations and ethnicities—Syrians, Lebanese, Greeks, Israelis, Philistines, Romans, and more—all passed through Capernaum and the surrounding area. The Gospel Triangle was multicultural and multiethnic, where people spoke more than one language, and where people went in search of health, relief, work, and prosperity.

But perhaps the area was best known for its profound spiritual darkness. It is possible this was the most important reason Jesus settled there for a time. It's clear that Jesus exercised a powerful and diverse ministry in this place to fulfill Isaiah's prophecy:

> Nevertheless, there will be no more gloom for those who were in distress. . . . But in the future He will honor Galilee of the Gentiles, by the way of the sea, along the Jordan—The people walking in darkness have seen a great light; on those living in the land of the shadow of death a light has dawned. (Isaiah 9:1–2)

Despite the healing waters, the commercial prosperity, and the rich cultural and ethnic diversities, spiritual darkness reigned in this area. The land occupied by Zebulun and Naphtali, two of the ancient tribes of Israel that had settled in that region, was the first to suffer the attacks of their enemy to the northeast, Syria. In addition, it was the constant host to the Greek pagan culture, which had a negative influence on the Jewish believers. They could not see clearly that God was the true God. Nor could they find an answer to the loneliness and suffering, the desolation of wars, the attacks of thieves, and the diversity of religious teachings that didn't get them anywhere.

What darkness! What a dead-end road!

Matthew says, "The people living in darkness have seen a great light" (Matthew 4:16). Walking in darkness is a serious problem. You can't see the wells, the stones, or even the road. There is no set course, just a mere wandering through life with no direction. That's how many of the people living in and passing through the Gospel Triangle were living. Light was just what they needed. Matthew doesn't say that the people saw a little light so that they felt a certain relief in finding part of the way. He says that the people "have seen a great light," and that "a light has dawned" (Matthew 4:16). The light was so bright that it illuminated the sins of the people so they could see them with all their great horror. But more than anything, with Jesus by their side, the people could see with complete clarity the love of the heavenly Father, His good will toward them, to forgive all without asking anything, and to give them strength to live life fully, in peace and joy.

Jesus' mission was not to just encourage people to find a better way of life. His mission was, on the contrary, to present Himself as the way (John 14:6) and as the light (John 8:12), so that whoever believed in Him might experience a radical change in their lives. God wants His creatures to be just like Jesus. Paul says that God wants to build us up until we "become mature, attaining to the whole measure of the fullness of Christ" (Ephesians 4:13).

It is no little thing that God wants to work in us. He has ambitious plans for His children. Perhaps that is why the people of Nazareth had such a hard time believing in Him. They just couldn't understand such radical changes. They, like many others, only looked for immediate and superficial relief. God, on the other hand, wants to give us a profound and eternal peace.

The Way of the Sea, the two languages, and the commercial traffic were, among others, the elements God used so that word about Jesus' preaching and acts of mercy, of healing and setting people free, might spread rapidly. The Gospel Triangle was an excellent strategic place for God's mission and for the fulfillment of Isaiah's prophecy. Jesus didn't choose by chance the places where He would carry out His mission. He didn't choose a place because He was comfortable or uncomfortable with the people or with the location. When He temporarily settled in Capernaum, it was to fulfill God's plan that He had established centuries before. Jesus always worked according to God's plan. After all, that is why He had come—to fulfill the Scriptures and to carry out the Father's will:

> I have come that they may have life, and have it to the full. (John 10:10)

Jesus affirms this. Many in Nazareth, Jerusalem, and the Gospel Triangle didn't understand these words. But there were many others who did understand and believed in Jesus, who lived to the full, and today in eternity live a life more blessed than we can imagine.

Read Isaiah 9:1–7.

Think about how Jesus fulfilled this prophecy.

Read John 1:6–12.

How did the Gospel writer John announce the mission of John the Baptist as well as Jesus' mission?

Map 4

The Gospel Triangle
N
Korazin
Bethsaida
Capernaum
Magdala
Sea *of*
Galilee
Tiberias
Country *of the* Gerasenes
Jordan River

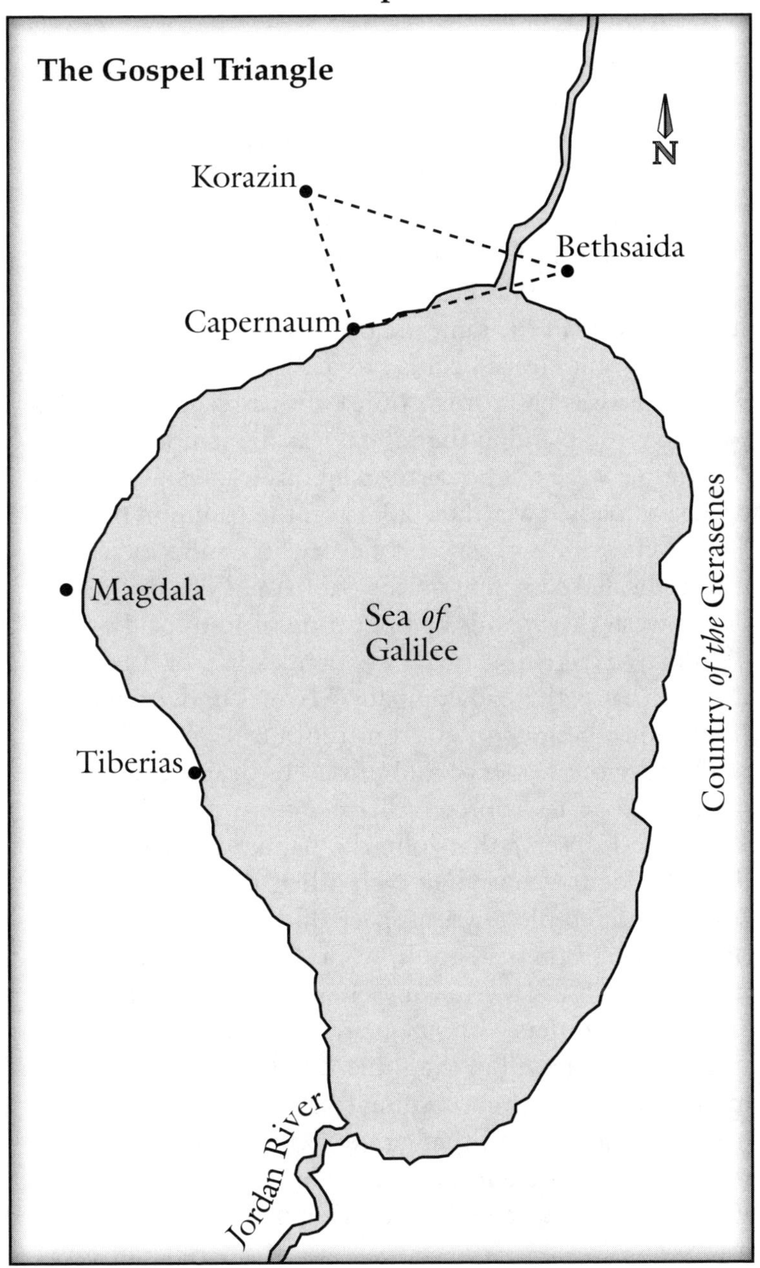

Part 3:
Where Do We Go?

As John the Baptist preached in the area of the Jordan, Jesus stayed in Judea, respecting the space and ministry of the Baptist. It is as if there was not a place for two such strong leaders in the same area. But when John disappears from the scene, Jesus begins His activities in Galilee.

Galilee was better than Judea in that respect. In Judea was the capital, and in the capital was the temple, and in the temple were the powerful religious leaders who "tie[d] up heavy loads" (Matthew 23:4) on the common people. They were critical observers of every little movement: if Jesus healed someone on the Sabbath, if His disciples didn't wash their hands before eating, if Jesus paid or didn't pay His temple tax, if He drank wine, or if He sat down to eat with "bad company." Now I understand why Jesus didn't hesitate to go from Judea to Galilee. The zeal of the religious leaders could cause His death. It was better for Him to go to a different place.

When I observe that John the Baptist and Jesus didn't hinder or contradict each other, when I see how Jesus respected the physical space of the ministry of the other leader, I think about how God places His leaders in the Church today. I see myself avoiding hypercritical, faultfinding leaders who safeguard a religion based on traditions not found in the Bible. I see that God has placed me where He sees fit according to His plan, where I am needed. I have had to change my style of ministry more than once. He has put me in a pulpit and in a lecture hall; He has sent me to counsel and comfort, to write and to listen.

The models God has for different ministries in His Church are not rigid, they are functional. But the message doesn't change. The message is the same one proclaimed by John the Baptist and by Jesus Himself:

> Repent, for the kingdom of heaven is near. (Matthew 4:17)

This phrase alone perfectly summarizes the whole message of God. "Repent." God looks at us and says, "Be aware of where you are. Take a good look at yourself. Look at how many sins you need forgiven! Look at your own misery, your needs, your frustrations, and that poor vision for your life that leads you through this world as a victim of circumstance, taking away your joy and peace. Take an honest look at your own life situation."

When we see ourselves as God sees us, John the Baptist and Jesus tell us, "The kingdom of heaven is near."

Here again, the words of the angel Gabriel are fulfilled as he announced that Jesus would be *Immanuel*, "God with us." That is definitely my ministry, to announce that God is with us. Where do I need to announce it? Wherever He may take me. Sometimes He makes me return to my hometown, to the people who watched me grow up. Thank heaven they never treat me like the people of Nazareth treated Jesus! Other times He's taken me to very poor places where more experienced leaders had to be patient with me and teach me to do a ministry for which there were no models. Other times I followed the traditional ways of the Church, very appropriate for some places, but not for others. Today I'm waiting to see—maybe God is designing a new ministry for me. I try to keep myself open to His will.

Observing the ministry of Jesus, of John the Baptist, and of the Church in general throughout history, I see that God has no limits. Actually, He dares us to step outside the limits we impose on ourselves. We have to step outside our own culture and accept another. We keep ourselves in our traditions without considering others, or we simply discount others who don't live the way we do. We impose geographical, social, racial, and religious limits on ourselves. We forget what Paul said in his Letter to the Galatians:

> There is neither Jew nor Greek, slave nor free, male nor female, for you are all one in Christ Jesus. (Galatians 3:28)

Jesus didn't have barriers when it came to reaching people. He stepped beyond the territorial limits of Israel, and He gave the same amount of attention to women and children as He did to men, something completely shocking in those days. The people of Nazareth didn't like the fact that God was so open and willing to be close to non-Jews. They believed more in themselves and their institutionalized religion than in God. That is why Matthew says categorically:

> [Jesus] did not do many miracles there because of their lack of faith. (Matthew 13:58)

The miracles weren't just to create a temporary well-being or to make Jesus famous. Rather, they were to show that Jesus was the Son of God and to create faith in His redemptive mission. If there was unbelief, there were no miracles.

I still can't understand why God doesn't perform miracles in "my own land," in my life, in my family, in the everyday things that could use some immediate relief. I'm not an unbeliever, but sometimes I forget that the real purpose of miracles is to reaffirm that Jesus is the Lord of my life. Matthew says:

> Then Jesus began to denounce the cities in which most of His miracles had been performed, because they did not repent. (Matthew 11:20)

Perhaps that's the part I fail to appreciate about the miracles of God—how many He's done in my life and in the lives of those around me. Miracles are to help me realize:

- Where I stand;
- Who I am;
- What I need;
- My sins;
- My hurts and pains; and
- My mortality.

When I realize all that, it produces repentance, and then I understand that I need God because I cannot overcome my hurts and sufferings, my sin, or my mortality by myself. There's where a great miracle happens! It's not very spectacular, but it's profound enough to change my life:

- The kingdom of heaven draws near.
- God comes and forgives me.
- He continues ruling my life with more authority than before.

And finally:

- The relief is not just circumstantial.

A great miracle God performed in my life was to give me new sight. In other words, He taught me to see not only with my eyes, but also with my heart. For a long time, I overspiritualized the message of Scripture. I thought that the blind were only those who couldn't see their sins and their need for God; that the prisoners were those trapped by their sins; that the sick were spiritually sick. It was a very comfortable way of looking at things. But the passage from Isaiah that Jesus read in Nazareth opened my eyes and softened my heart to see that God rules all the spheres of life, not just the spiritual.

Today I'm waiting expectantly for new miracles, hoping to see new things. I like it when God surprises me.

Read Matthew 11:20–24.

Think about the judgment Jesus pronounced over the cities of the Gospel Triangle.

Think about a miracle that has strengthened your faith.

Chapter 6

Part 1:
Jesus' Relationship with the Father

Some people suffer shame and frustration because they don't know who their father is. They feel ashamed because they were born out of an illegitimate relationship, and they feel frustrated because there's an emptiness in their identity that is hard to fill. Knowing where you come from is of vital importance. It gives you a sense of belonging and the security that you are part of something that will continue. Generally, when you don't know where you come from, you don't know where you're going, and the sense of shame and frustration becomes sharper.

When the evangelist Matthew writes about Jesus, the first thing he does is list Jesus' ancestors (Matthew 1:1–16) in order to establish His identity. God knows that it is important to know where one comes from, and that's why He took scrupulous care with the genealogical line of His Son.

What is interesting here is that even though Joseph was only Jesus' adoptive father, and even though he is only mentioned during Jesus' infancy, he probably had plenty of time to educate Jesus and to impress his character on Him. The evangelist Luke tells us that Jesus' parents took Him to Jerusalem every year for the Passover. Those must have been unforgettable family experiences. Joseph is mentioned for the last time in one of those trips, when Jesus was twelve years old and stayed in Jerusalem to take care of His Father's business (Luke 2:39). This is the last time that Joseph, Jesus' adoptive father, is mentioned, and it's the first time that Jesus talks about His Father in heaven.

Identifying Jesus with Joseph and with all His ancestors, principally with David and Abraham, was very important. But for Jesus, there is now a change. It is necessary for Him to begin little by little to point out His identity with the heavenly Father. Perhaps His earthly parents didn't fully understand what kind of business Jesus had to be about with His Father, but:

> [Mary] treasured all these things in her heart. (Luke 2:51)

For Jesus, the connection with the Father was essential if He wanted to carry out the enormous task of saving mankind. Knowing where He came from helped Him stay focused on His final destiny. He said so to His disciples:

> I came from the Father and entered the world; now I am leaving the world and going back to the Father. (John 16:28)

During His entire ministry, Jesus was clearly identified with His Father. Really, that was one of the objectives of His work: to show the Father. In one of His final meetings with His disciples before His death, Jesus emphatically told Philip:

> Anyone who has seen Me has seen the Father. (John 14:9)

Today we would say of Jesus and the Father, "Like Father, like Son"—the same character, the same goodness, the same compassion, the same authority, the same passion for saving the lost, the same toughness toward hypocrites, the same origin, the same loving vocation of restoring creation. Like Father, like Son.

The Gospels record several occasions when Jesus looked for a way to maintain His intimate communion with the Father:

> Very early in the morning, while it was still dark, Jesus got up, left the house and went off to a solitary place, where He prayed. (Mark 1:35)

This happened just moments before Simon found Him and took Him to a place where a crowd was looking for Him. But Jesus decided to leave those who were looking for Him and go to other places to preach. His connection with the Father kept Him focused on His ministry. He didn't let Himself get carried away by the urgency of the situation or the insistence of the people. Another time, after having fed more than five thousand people, Matthew relates:

> Immediately Jesus made the disciples get into the boat . . . while He dismissed the crowd. After He had dismissed them, He went up on a mountainside by Himself to pray. (Matthew 14:22–23)

Admirable! Prayer is no excuse for not working. Jesus didn't leave things unattended. He first put His disciples in the boat and sent them to the other side of the lake, then He dismissed the crowd. Only then did He look for a solitary place where He could be with His Father to refocus Himself on His mission.

The apostle John adds an interesting detail to this situation. After Jesus performed the miracle of feeding five thousand people, everyone realized that Jesus was truly the prophet who was to come into the world, but

> Jesus, knowing that they intended to come and make Him king by force, withdrew again to a mountain by Himself. (John 6:15)

Jesus didn't let the crowd's plans change His objective. He immediately went to a solitary place to get recharged with the Father's power and to refocus on His work. It wasn't about following the agenda of His admirers, but following the mission the Father had entrusted to Him.

That's what He also did the night He was betrayed. Matthew describes in rich detail the presence of Jesus before His Father: His sweat, like great drops of blood; His goings and comings, asking the disciples to be with Him during that final hour; His prostrating Himself on the ground; and His anxiety, sadness, and supplication. So His own prophecy was fulfilled:

> But a time is coming, and has come, when you will be scattered, each to his own home. You will leave Me all alone. Yet I am not alone, for My Father is with Me. (John 16:32)

His friends left Him alone, overcome by sleep. Later on, overcome by fear, they left Him alone again. But the Father was always with Him. Or nearly always, because there is one moment in Jesus' life, the moment of His greatest pain, when His Father abandoned Him. Jesus hangs on a cross after having suffered the vilest injustice of the Jews. He suffers abandonment by His friends, the intolerance of the religious leaders, and the hate of those who were frustrated with Him. But His cry wasn't directed toward any of them. Neither did He reproach those who crucified Him. On the contrary, His cry of anguish was directed toward His Father, who had abandoned Him: "Dad! Dad! Why do You leave Me?"

The Father had His reasons for momentarily abandoning Jesus to be swallowed up by death. He had to die alone. He had to experience the pain of being without His Father.

But the promises still remained. Jesus knew by heart the promises that His Father had made. He would come back from death and would reign over the whole universe (Mark 16:19). And just as He always did, the Father kept His promises. Jesus was once again reunited with His Father.

The apostle Paul explains this abandonment and reunion of Jesus with His Father when he writes to the Philippians:

> He humbled Himself and became obedient to death—even death on a cross! Therefore God exalted Him to the highest place and gave Him the name that is above every name, that at the name of Jesus every knee should bow, in heaven and on earth and under the earth, and every tongue confess that Jesus Christ is Lord, to the glory of God the Father. (Philippians 2:8–11)

Read John 14.

Describe the extent of the relationship of Jesus with His Father.

Part 2:
Jesus Teaches Us to Be with the Father

James: Simon, have you seen the Teacher? I've looked everywhere, but I can't find Him.

Simon: He left early while it was still dark outside. He probably went out to pray again.

James: To pray again? It hasn't been long since He disappeared for the whole night to be alone. I've never seen anyone invest so much time in prayer.

Simon: It must do Him good, because every time He comes back from prayer, He looks transformed, full of energy, ready to go out and preach and heal the sick.

James: I've noticed that His way of praying is different from other religious leaders', who stand on the street corners so the entire world can see them. Jesus almost always goes someplace where He can be alone.

Simon: Maybe we could ask Him to teach us how to pray. I think we could learn more from Him than we learned in the synagogue.

James: But what we learned at the synagogue isn't bad!

Simon: Of course not! But it looks to me like the Teacher experiences something different in His prayer time. Remember when the seventy returned from their missionary campaign? I've never seen anyone as happy as Jesus was. He openly and joyfully expressed Himself before God the Father (Luke 10:21–24). His prayer times must really be enriching.

Simon had to bite his tongue because he knew much more than he could tell his friend. He'd been with Jesus and two other disciples at the time when Jesus was transformed completely while praying:

> As He was praying, the appearance of His face changed, and His clothes became as bright as a flash of lightning. (Luke 9:29)

Although for Simon it had been one of his most intimate moments with Jesus, during which he and his friends had seen things no one had ever experienced before, he couldn't say anything about it. He remembered the Teacher's words quite well:

> As they were coming down the mountain, Jesus instructed them, "Don't tell anyone what you have seen, until the Son of Man has been raised from the dead." (Matthew 17:9)

Perhaps it would be best, Simon thought, to ask Jesus directly to teach them how to pray. He just had to wait for the right moment to ask.

And he didn't have to wait long for that moment:

> One day Jesus was praying in a certain place. When He finished, one of His disciples said to Him, "Lord, teach us to pray, just as John taught his disciples." (Luke 11:1)

Jesus' answer covered three areas:

- The form and practice,
- The content, and
- The promise.

When Matthew writes about Jesus' teachings on prayer, he begins with a practical question because, for Jesus, there are only two distinct ways of practicing religion. One way is to make oneself seen so that everyone can see how good and pious one is, as those in His day would do when they presented their offerings in front of everybody in order to be admired:

> Be careful not to do your "acts of righteousness" before men, to be seen by them. If you do, you will have no reward from your Father in heaven. (Matthew 6:1)
>
> And when you pray, do not be like the hypocrites, for they love to pray standing in the synagogues and on the street corners to be seen by men. I tell you the truth, they have received their reward in full. (Matthew 6:5)
>
> And when you pray, do not keep on babbling like pagans, for they think they will be heard because of their many words. (Matthew 6:7)

Surely this was a very common practice that was quite different from what the disciples saw in Jesus and even in John the Baptist (Luke 11:1).

The other way of practicing religion—and in this case, prayer, as Jesus taught—was to pray alone to God the Father. It isn't about reciting the rosary, but about concentrating privately in a private place and pouring out one's heart to the Father.

"Father" seems to be Jesus' preferred term when speaking with God—not "God of the Armies," not "God of Abraham, Isaac, and Jacob," as so often appears in the Old Testament, but simply "Father." With this word, Jesus begins to explain what a prayer should contain. On one hand, "Our Father" shows the attitude of God toward His children, when He asks us to call Him "Father." On the other hand, it sums up our basic needs. God doesn't want His children to lose focus. It was very easy for the disciples to get confused. The Pharisees prayed one way, and many others lived their religion in a way that was not taught or practiced by Jesus. It was so easy to lose the purpose! The disciples needed a clear and specific guide, and Jesus gave it to them:

"Keep the name of God in the highest esteem. It is the most important thing there is. It is holy and does not mix with impure and sinful things. Keep it away from anything frivolous or impetuous. Respect it as that of your own father. Ask God to open your eyes to see His good will toward the whole world. God wants you to know about His passion for the sick and suffering, for the lost, and that His good will is that everyone in the world should be saved from eternal catastrophe. Be willing to live according to God's will. Ask for what you need for each day and nothing more. Don't worry about tomorrow. And remember:

> I am the bread of life. He who comes to Me will never go hungry, and he who believes in Me will never be thirsty. (John 6:35)

"You will need Me every day in order to be spiritually well nourished. Ask the Father not to take your sins into account. The forgiveness of God is the only thing that can set you free from the bonds of conscience, from sins and errors. There's no other way to get rid of them. Forgive those who offend you so that your mind will not be occupied by seeking revenge and so you don't become bitter. Show your neighbors the freedom that God's forgiveness brings. In this world you will have many temptations. You will be tempted not to forgive and to believe that the sins of others against you are greater than your sins against others and against God. Don't give in to that or any other temptation. Remember that evil is present everywhere and that the devil is constantly looking to separate people from God. Fervently ask the Father to deliver you from every evil, because you will not have the spiritual and emotional strength needed to free yourselves. Only the Father can keep you from every evil."

After teaching them how to pray, Jesus reassured His disciples of God's willingness to hear and attend to their prayers. Through various examples Jesus encouraged them to trust that God pays profound attention to the needs we present to Him in private:

> Which of you fathers, if your son asks for a fish, will give him a snake instead? . . . How much more will your Father in heaven give the Holy Spirit to those who ask Him! (Luke 11:11, 13)

This promise would bring the disciples together with the first believers to meet every day in homes to break bread, to be in communion, and to pray. In this way, they were able to face temptations and hatred, and they grew in numbers and in the joy of the Holy Spirit (Acts 2:42; 4:31).

Read Matthew 7:7–12.

Find at least three main points that Jesus teaches about prayer.

Read Matthew 6:5–8.

How can this passage be applied to your own religious life today?

Part 3:
I'm Still Learning

I get along well with my parents. I believe it's a privilege and a great blessing, especially when I observe the problems between children and their parents in today's society. My children tell me that I'm looking more like their grandfather all the time—the same haircut, the same way of walking, the same expressions, even the same illnesses! Perhaps they are saying to me, "Like father, like son."

Undoubtedly my parents impressed their character on me. It can be seen in my way of thinking and especially in the way I live my faith. For example, I learned from my parents that you don't play with God. God is a serious matter.

Perhaps this is the greatest legacy I received from my ancestors. The testimony of my parents' faith molded my character and prepared me to face whatever came up in my life.

Every year I went with my parents to celebrate the Resurrection (*la Pascua de la Resurección*) . . . thirty feet from my home. I didn't go alone. My brother and my two sisters were also there, but we didn't stay afterward to discuss Scriptures with the teachers of the Law. We would go back to the kitchen, fighting among ourselves for whatever reason. But these religious activities, Easter, Christmas, Thanksgiving, as well as every Sunday's worship services, were unforgettable experiences of family and faith. My first formative years in the arms of my earthly parents marked the beginning of my communion with my heavenly Father.

I didn't learn or practice, until fairly recently, to be alone with the Father in a quiet place. But even before that, I usually consulted with the Father in heaven before facing any new task or taking a new step in my life. Sadly, I didn't always do so, and it showed in the results. When I concentrated on intimacy with the Father, my heart beat slower with a more appropriate rhythm. When I poured out my troubled spirit before God, inevitably Jesus' promise was fulfilled:

> The Father will give you whatever you ask in My name. (John 15:16)

Of course, it took time to learn God's timing and to submit to His will. Actually, learning to pray and receive God's answer took me longer than I would have liked. I'm still learning! I often stray from my purpose and find myself concentrating on the immediate moment and what affects me personally. I have trouble seeing the needs of others. I have poor spiritual vision when it comes to seeing how God's plan fits in my life and my family's life.

Many times I let myself get carried along by the Church's agenda rather than God's agenda. Other times, I stop working to pray, but many more times I stop praying because I don't have enough time to finish all I had planned to do in a day. I am ashamed to be so far from living in intimacy with the Father as Jesus did. I've never had an experience like Peter, James, and John had when they went to the top of the mount with Jesus and witnessed His transfiguration. It was such a sublime moment that Peter wanted to stay and live there (Matthew 17:4).

But perhaps my intimacy with the Father grows in a different way. I believe that the mountaintop for me is when I read the Bible. I love to read the Scriptures because God always surprises me with new things He wants to reveal to me, and in most cases, it has an immediate application in my life. God never ceases to surprise me. He's capable of turning me back to my purpose every time I lose sight of it. I realize that on my own, I cannot live a full and healthy life that takes God's whole mission into account. Invariably I need God to help me concentrate on what He has called me to do.

I'm not in the habit of vain repetitions. I don't pray the rosary, because I'm not Roman Catholic, but neither do I repeat the Lord's Prayer every day or any other written prayer. I'm not proud of this, and I hope no one follows my example, but I don't feel uncomfortable because of it. As I said before, I believe that my mountaintop experience with the Father happens more while reading Scriptures than in reciting prayers.

One time, a few years ago, I did as Jesus said:

> But when you pray, go into your room, close the door and pray to your Father, who is unseen. (Matthew 6:6)

It wasn't the only time I went to my room to pray alone (I still do it with certain regularity), but I remember that particular occasion. I went into my room, pulled down the shades to make it dark, lay on the bed, relaxing my body, and thought about one of my favorite Old Testament passages:

> But those who hope in the Lord will renew their strength. They will soar on wings like eagles; they will run and not grow weary, they will walk and not be faint. (Isaiah 40:31)

Then I began to imagine how it would feel to ride on an eagle, and I believe I lost all awareness of my surroundings. I saw myself riding the eagle as one would ride a horse. We flew smoothly to incredible heights, the eagle moving its wings in a slow steady rhythm. I wasn't scared at all. On the contrary, I felt as if I were part of the eagle. I could see everything from that great height. We skimmed the peaks of the highest mountains, we breathed lighter, more pristine air, and there were no noises to disturb us. I imagined it was God's eagle that carried me on a high and smooth flight through life.

I don't know when I got off the eagle, or when the flight ended. All I know is that since then, Isaiah's words took on a whole new meaning for me. Perhaps on that day, God wanted to give me a little part of the transfiguration experience that Peter, James, and John lived, so I could feel more encouraged in the presence of the Father and have "renewed strength" to spread "wings like eagles."

I discovered that God doesn't want us to be like other birds He created—for example, parrots, which only mechanically repeat sounds that have no meaning to them. God created us to be like eagles, to fly high and have a wide vision of the reality here below, while experiencing His peace in the heights.

Perhaps what I need to reconsider time and again about prayer is to let God take me where He wants to take me. I realize I'm very covetous of my own life. I don't feel like getting on God's eagle and letting it carry me away. It suits me to stay here below and make only little hops. I don't stop to realize that God wants to take me to other heights to give me a better view of life.

Invariably, after an intimate moment with my heavenly Father, I leave strengthened, prepared to face my daily tasks, focused on God's plan, and rested from my worries. I'm encouraged by His promise that He will care for me and give me everything I need for a joyful life.

Read Matthew 6:25–33.

Relate this Bible passage to what Jesus teaches about prayer.

Think about a prayer experience you have had that was out of the ordinary.

Chapter 7

Part 1:
The Teaching of Jesus
(Matthew 5:13–48)

"Where does He get such wisdom and miracles?" the people asked themselves after listening to Jesus in the synagogue at Nazareth. The Gospel writers tell us many times that Jesus went to the synagogues to teach (Matthew 4:23). Surely He spent time in the synagogues at first to learn, just as He spent time alone with the Father to reaffirm everything He had learned in the Scriptures. Jesus knew the Scriptures so well that when He had to refute the devil during the temptation, He quoted them without hesitation.

When Jesus opened His mouth to teach, surely everyone remained silent. "No one ever spoke like this man!" the guards told the Pharisees. The guards had gone to arrest Jesus, but He convinced them with His teaching! Instead of arresting Him, they were left standing with their mouths open, completely impressed by Jesus' words (John 7:32, 46). But the guards were not the only ones impressed by Jesus' teaching. After Jesus finished preaching on the mountain:

> The crowds were amazed at His teaching, because He taught as one who had authority, and not as their teachers of the law. (Matthew 7:28–29)

That must have been one of the reasons why Jesus was so popular and respected among the people. The scribes and Pharisees were not the best examples of virtue, so they were not admired among the people. Jesus once told the people to fulfill what the Pharisees taught them but to not imitate them, because they imposed heavy loads on the people without moving a finger themselves (Matthew 23:3–4).

The rabbis had divided the Law into 613 commandments and spent their time interpreting them and making sure the people obeyed them. Jesus summarized God's Law in just two commandments: love God and love your neighbor (Matthew 22:37–40).

The Pharisees laid heavy burdens on the people. Jesus brought them rest and relief from their burdens and troubles (Matthew 11:28).

Jesus didn't only teach with words, but also with actions. Jesus' teaching touched people's hearts. They were practical things that affected the people's relationship with God and with one another.

During those times, it was customary to follow the law of recompense established in the Old Testament that applied a punishment equal to the harm that had been done:

- "If you steal my horse, I will steal yours."
- "If you hit me on the cheek, I will return the blow."

- "An eye for an eye, and a tooth for a tooth."

Moses had taught the people to live this way to avoid extreme vengeance. But Jesus has a different idea as to how God's society should be, and He taught the people not to return evil for evil, but to practice love:

> If someone forces you to go one mile, go with him two miles. (Matthew 5:41)

It seemed like a new teaching, but it really wasn't.

- What was Jesus getting at?
- What did He want to accomplish with His teaching?
- Was He contradicting Moses?

Jesus had specific goals when He preached and taught:

- that the people would recognize their sin and come to God for forgiveness;
- that those who heard Him would undergo a change in their lives for the better; and
- that those who learned from Him could live their new lives to the fullest and pass that benefit on to their community.

Jesus' teaching was radical and different from the teaching of the rabbis. Jesus put the Father forward as an example: If God makes the sun shine on the good and the bad, you have to treat everyone well, good or bad. But Jesus gets to the climax when He says:

> Be perfect, therefore, as your heavenly Father is perfect. (Matthew 5:48)

The word "perfect" that Jesus uses here comes from the original Greek *telos*, which has a very broad meaning, and which is translated here as "full" or "mature." The Greek word *telos* can mean a theatrical curtain or backdrop. When a play is done, the curtain comes down, and we know the play is over; there is no more. So Jesus proposes that we come to absolute fullness and maturity, until, in the end, we are fully and completely mature as our Father in heaven is fully and completely mature.

The last words of Jesus on the cross were these:

> It is finished. (John 19:30)

The word "finished" is based on the Greek word *telos*. It is as if before He died, Jesus was saying, "The curtain is down. The work is complete. The salvation of humankind was perfectly finished. There is nothing else to add."

When Jesus proposed that we be perfect (*telos*) as the Father in heaven is perfect, He is telling us to be full and mature, to go the extra mile, to take an extra step toward keeping the Law, to love others as He did to the point of giving His own life. Jesus kept the Law to perfection, but it was that extra mile that saved us. It was His voluntary offering of Himself on the cross that defeated Satan and won eternal freedom for us. If Jesus had returned blow for blow, we would not have been saved. If Jesus, in His own righteousness, had defended Himself against those who handed Him over to suffer, we would not have been saved. If Jesus had applied the Law according to the rules and regulations of the rabbis, He wouldn't have gone to the cross. If He had not gone to the cross, He wouldn't have been raised from the dead. If He had not been raised from the dead, we would still be condemned by our own sins (1 Corinthians 15:17).

But Jesus fulfilled the Law according to the Father's will, walking the extra mile, and so He changed our lives. That was the characteristic of the life He lived "to perfection," in fullness and maturity. This kind of life changes the lives of those around it, making a positive impact for the good of others.

Walking the extra mile, not exercising the law of recompense, not paying eye for eye, tooth for tooth, is not a way of making oneself feel better, but something we do so blessing might spread through the community around us.

Doing so, by the power of the Holy Spirit, we will reach that perfection to which God has called us. The apostle Paul really understood these concepts and applied them in his Letter to the Ephesians when he said that God provided the way that "the body of Christ may be built up until we all reach unity in the faith and in the knowledge of the Son of God and become mature [*telos*], attaining to the whole measure of the fullness of Christ" (Ephesians 4:12–13).

We need to realize that God wants the best for us. His goal is for us to arrive at the final curtain, that we live a life to which there is nothing to add, that we live in such a way that we attain the stature of the fullness of Christ. Nothing more, nothing less. This is the objective of Jesus' teaching. And to all this we must add that our "final curtain" doesn't come down here, but when God culminates His work by taking us to heaven. There, perfection will have a dimension that we can only vaguely imagine while in this world.

Read Matthew 5:25–48.

Think about the "new way" Jesus interpreted the Law.

What is your reaction to the Greek concept of *telos*, perfect, mature, and full?

Part 2:
Jesus Teaches through Parables
(Matthew 13:1–50)

Many times the disciples, among others, called Jesus "Teacher" or "Rabbi." Jesus was a school in Himself that taught as much by example as by His mighty works and words. However, we need to understand that Jesus' main work was not teaching, but saving. He came to fulfill God's Law, to die and rise again to save humankind. Jesus was not only a great liberator like Moses, and a great teacher admired by multitudes for His wisdom, but above all, He was the Lamb of God who took away the sin of the world. That's how John the Baptist presented Him. The lamb was an animal well known to the Israelites. A sacrificial lamb was also well known to the Hebrews, since they regularly sacrificed lambs to receive forgiveness for their sins, in addition to eating a lamb every year during the Passover feast. What a parable John the Baptist used to present the Son of God! The lamb was a figurative way of presenting Jesus. This had great significance to those who knew the Scriptures and related Jesus, the Lamb, to the Old Testament passages, especially Isaiah 52 and 53.

Jesus was a parable in Himself and often used parables to teach. A parable is a form of teaching with illustrations that had purposes that were almost contradictory. Jesus puts Himself at the same level as the crowds and uses well-known images, with the goal of making the people see new things, or see things from a new point of view. Matthew says that Jesus, teaching with parables, fulfilled the prophecy that says:

> I will open My mouth in parables, I will utter things hidden since the creation of the world. (Matthew 13:35)

Among the images Jesus used were daily things known to everyone, such as money; yeast; a seed; a treasure; fish; nets; fruit; a pearl; sheep; men and women doing different jobs; and activities such as weddings, banquets, sowing, and harvesting.

You can imagine that Jesus' parables gave people something to talk about. Many times, people would gather after listening to Him to try and discover the hidden things He had spoken of in the parable. But generally, the listeners couldn't understand the parables. Not even His own disciples understood what their Master was trying to teach them. After Jesus told the parable of the weeds, His disciples asked:

> Explain to us the parable of the weeds in the field. (Matthew 13:36)

This doesn't mean that God didn't want to open the ears and change the hearts of the people. What it means is that Jesus understood and accepted the reality of His time, that many of His listeners didn't really want to learn from Him or to know of God and His plans. The parables in themselves were not that difficult, but there is a secret to understanding them: being with Jesus. The Gospel writer Mark says of Jesus:

> He did not say anything to them without using a parable. But when He was alone with His own disciples, He explained everything. (Mark 4:34)

Oh, what a blessing! Only the chosen ones had the privilege of knowing the "secrets" of the kingdom of heaven, the plans of God. Categorically, Jesus affirmed to the Twelve and the others around Him:

> The secret of the kingdom of God has been given to you. But to those on the outside everything is said in parables. (Mark 4:10–11)

Each parable has at least one basic teaching that God wants to convey, although many are abundant in details that enrich the main content. It's noteworthy that a good number of parables begin with the phrase "The kingdom of heaven is similar to . . . ." Jesus used parables to explain how the Father's will is carried out on earth, what the kingdom of God is among us, how we can recognize it, how we can make it grow, and what we can hope for in that kingdom. The kingdom of heaven is a new and extraordinary thing, so big that it encompasses all areas of life. It cannot be described in a single parable. That's why Jesus used so many.

Matthew has a collection of brief parables in chapter 13, among which is the parable of the net (vv. 47–50). Surely all of the disciples and many other people in the area were very familiar with fishing. Some of Jesus' followers were professional fishermen. They earned their living fishing. They knew very well what a net was. They washed nets, mended them, and got them ready to go out again into the lake to fish. They also knew fish—which ones were good for salting and selling and which ones to throw back into the water because they weren't edible.

Those who were with Jesus also knew that there's a time to classify or separate the fish. Obviously that can't be done while the fish are in the water. The fisherman cannot get out of the boat in the middle of the lake, separate the good fish from the bad fish, and put all the ones he wants to catch in one place and throw away those he cannot use. That would be impossible! The fisherman has to pull in the net, take out all the fish, and then separate them. Fishermen also know that the fish do not separate themselves. That is the work of the fisherman.

In this way, using activities and elements well known to His listeners, Jesus taught that in the kingdom of heaven, the forgiven and the unforgiven live together. There is no physical way to separate them. The Gospel cannot be preached only to those whom we think could be saved. Neither should we keep the Gospel from those who seem useless or beyond saving to the community. When Judgment Day comes, God will fish for all; His net will be finely woven and all will be brought to shore. There, God's angels will sort us. We will not sort ourselves. No one will be able to choose where to go. Only God has that authority. He is the experienced Fisherman who knows who is clean and who is not.

At the end of the parable, Jesus speaks very clearly:

> This is how it will be at the end of the age. The angels will come and separate the wicked from the righteous and throw them into the fiery furnace, where there will be weeping and gnashing of teeth. (Matthew 13:49–50)

It was surely with profound pain that Jesus pronounced such a harsh sentence. But as we have already seen, Jesus did not waver from telling the truth. He wasn't afraid of wounding sensitive spirits or hypocrites. On the contrary, He wanted to call them to repentance so that at the end of time, when God casts His net into the sea of humanity, He might find more people justified by the Savior than those who must be thrown into the fire.

That is what the kingdom of God is like: a kingdom hoping for a great catch, where all, indistinguishable and inseparable, share the same sun and rain that God sends to everyone equally (Matthew 5:45).

Read Matthew 13:18–23.

See how this parable of the kingdom of God applies to our current time.

Read Matthew 13:24–30.

Relate this parable to the parable of the net in Matthew 13:47–50.

Part 3:
Jesus Showed Me a Different Way

Ah, perfection. How I would love to be perfect . . . in my own way! And I've tried! But my way of being perfect doesn't work. On the contrary, it's extremely frustrating. I tried to be a perfect son, and my parents often reminded me that even with severe discipline, I wasn't perfect. I tried to be the perfect husband, but I didn't even come close. I won't even attempt to say I tried to be the perfect father because my children remind me over and over that perfection done my way is really pretty imperfect. The thing is, my perfection is founded in the law of equal retribution. I don't tolerate being hit because I don't hit anyone, at least not physically. If someone makes me tow their car for one mile, I do exactly that and not a foot more because I can't stand being forced into doing anything. After all, it is much easier on me to love someone who loves me and ignore someone who hates me. It's easier to loan something to someone who I know can pay me back.

Recently I learned the meaning of "the extra mile," to go beyond the limits of the Law. For a long time, I thought that fullness and maturity came from strictly keeping the Law. I measured people, but not by their capacity to forgive or to understand and tolerate the impertinence of others or to love selflessly. It seemed stupid to me that people would not demand to be repaid money they had loaned, or would not strike back when offended. Only when I understood Jesus' extra step, loving me all the way to the cross even though He didn't have to do it, did I learn the way of perfection.

I am perfect when I walk toward maturity, when I don't measure the miles I have to walk with someone who is hurt, and when I don't return evil for evil. After listening to Jesus on this subject, this passage from Paul makes sense:

> If your enemy is hungry, feed him; if he is thirsty, give him something to drink. In doing this, you will heap burning coals on his head. (Romans 12:20)

Love and good deeds are superior to evil and bad deeds. Many times my face has burned with shame because God has placed people along my way who love me more than I can imagine or measure, and who don't take into account my meanness and selfishness, but who accept me as I am and love me without limits. I have learned a lot from them, perhaps more than from any teacher or professor.

I also know that those who walked with me much more than the extra mile, until I could resume walking on my own, didn't do it by their own power. It was noticeable that they were always near to Jesus, that they understood His teachings, that they treasured His offering on the cross, and that they received their power from the Holy Spirit. None of us could ever walk in perfection or give ourselves to others without the power from on high.

Being righteous, perfect, or good isn't something I could accomplish on my own. I'm just another fish in troubled waters. It was the grace of God that reached me, and even though He didn't take me out of the water, He cleansed me and showed me a new way of life. Sometimes I feel so privileged to have been reached by God's grace that I get distracted and am unaware of the world in which I live.

But the parable of the net puts me back in place with others and weakens my tendency to separate myself. I don't want to have the bad fish among us. It frustrates me to see how the good and bad are mixed. It's hard for me to see so many sinners sharing in God's blessings along with the redeemed. "It's not fair," I think, and I want to do some quick sorting. I don't even have the patience to wait until Judgment Day. I attempt to know better than God Himself as to who should be in the kingdom of heaven and who shouldn't. As if I could do a better job than the angels! As if I had any authority to do such a thing! How I would like to be the judge! I closely resemble the older brother in the parable of the prodigal son (Luke 15:11–32).

Perhaps that is the most tender parable Jesus taught. He used the human element in its every dimension: an inexperienced son who wants to go out into the world; another, more mature son, hardworking and almost irreproachable; and a father who risks letting his sons make their own way in life.

Although there are only three people, many characteristics appear in the way they behave. One thing that I learn here is that people change, some for the better, some for the worse.

In the case of the younger brother, I can see that he wasn't interested in family. It didn't matter to him to be away from his loved ones or to waste what he had not earned himself. He thought that money would last forever and that he didn't need to pay attention to anyone. The younger son doesn't tell his father why he wants his share of the inheritance, but once he has it, he abandons his family. This is a characteristic attitude of many people. But money doesn't last forever, nor can it buy happiness forever. Only when he had hit bottom, having to feed pigs and covet their food, did he begin to reflect. He had to squander all his worldly goods in order to recognize how much he had when he was with his father. Then he changed and was ready to return home. He didn't attempt to regain his dignity or his position as son. He only wanted to buy food from his father. Now he realized what he had done and the pain he had caused his family.

The father's attitude was magnificent. He didn't change, just as God never changes His gesture of love for us. The father is waiting and watching, without demanding explanations or giving a reproach. That's how it is with our heavenly Father. He's always waiting for us, to hug and kiss us, to dress and adorn us with His jewels, and to satisfy our need for food, good relationships, and to celebrate with Him. He doesn't take into account the bad that we've done or how we've wasted His gifts. What interests Him most is that we are returned to His house in peace.

It's evident that we can be at home, but not in peace. It only takes a little while for rage and resentment to appear. Here is the difference between the father and the older son. The father forgave his younger son from the day he left, which is why he always waited anxiously for him, to the point that he had prepared an animal for his welcoming party. The older son couldn't forgive his brother's impudence, first, for having abandoned the family; second, for having sinfully wasted the family's goods; and third, for having the audacity to return.

I often think about this parable of Jesus, especially when situations come up that produce anger in me and bring back old resentments because I didn't forgive people who weren't perfect in my eyes. Sometimes I also identify with the younger son and am glad that God waits for me with arms wide open time and time again. There is nothing better than feeling His embrace and hearing his words of welcome.

This parable teaches me that there is nothing more important than being in a good relationship with the heavenly Father, who doesn't keep a record of wrongs that I do, and who doesn't scold or blame me when I come back, repentant. His house is always open for me.

Read Luke 15:11–32.

With which of the three people in the parable can you identify?

Chapter 8

Part 1: *Jesus Didn't Work Alone*

(Matthew 10:1–15)

Thomas: It isn't true. We know He was dead. If they took Him down from the cross and put Him inside a tomb, He can't be walking around. I've never heard of such a thing. Besides, the nails had to have broken His ankles. He couldn't possibly be walking around like you said He was.

James: The women saw Him first and told us about it. We thought they were crazy, that the Teacher's death had affected their minds.

Peter: Exactly—but then He appeared to us and showed us His wounds, and we saw that He was fine. He reproached us for doubting that He was alive, and He encouraged us to believe what the Scriptures say.

Thomas: Unless I see with my own eyes, I won't believe.

Peter: All that Jesus has said has been fulfilled. Sometimes we just don't understand it right away.

James: Now I believe. It was incredible how Jesus' words were fulfilled when He told you, Peter, that you would deny Him three times.

Peter: Why do you have to bring that up? As if you were better than me! You fell asleep that night in Gethsemane too! Why didn't you stay awake to pray with Him?

Thomas: Why are you talking about that now? If you fell asleep, it was because you were too tired. Following Jesus is totally exhausting! And besides, it's frustrating. Now He's dead, and all our dreams of freedom have gone up in smoke. James, your dreams and those of your mother and brother, of having a privileged place in Jesus' kingdom, have gone up in smoke (Matthew 20:20–24).

James: I thought we were done talking about this. Didn't you pay attention to what the Teacher said about our discipleship? I never thought that being Jesus' disciple would be so different from what we were used to seeing: that we're all equal, that we were called to serve and not to exercise authority over others. Following Jesus is fascinating, and now that He's risen from the dead, the best is yet to come.

James was right. The best was yet to come. Repeatedly, the Book of Acts says that the disciples were filled with the Holy Spirit and were bold and full of joy (Acts 4:31; 5:41; 13:52). Nothing could keep them from exercising their apostleship with joy; not persecution, nor the unbelief of many people, nor being misunderstood by the religious leaders, not even the death of Stephen (Acts 7). The disciples were well prepared. Jesus did a good job with them, because after His ascension, the disciples took the momentum of the Holy Spirit and preached the Gospel tirelessly.

Jesus never tried to do everything alone. From the beginning, He was supported by the work of John the Baptist. So great was His respect for John's ministry that Jesus waited until John was no longer in action before beginning His own ministry in Galilee. After His Baptism, Jesus began to meet with a group of followers. He called them one by one. And one by one, they all left behind their activities and followed Him without knowing clearly what He expected of them. In the Gospels, there is no record of any promise Jesus made to His disciples, such as "Follow Me and you won't have any more problems!" or "Follow Me and God will give you a special reward!" Rather, He simply said:

> Come, follow Me . . . and I will make you fishers of men. (Matthew 4:19)

Some characteristics of Jesus' call to His followers are worth mentioning. The disciples immediately left everything they were doing. There was no hesitation. On one occasion, some approached Jesus to follow Him, but without first separating themselves from their families or possessions. Jesus said to them:

> No one who puts his hand to the plow and looks back is fit for service in the kingdom of God. (Luke 9:62)

When following the Lord, there is no other way to look but forward.

There were others who followed Him for some time, but because they couldn't accept all of Jesus' teachings, they turned back (John 6:66). To be a disciple, you have to be available to learn the task.

According to Matthew, many people from all over followed Jesus because they were attracted by His powers and miracles. But being attracted is very different from being called. A disciple doesn't follow Jesus because he feels attracted and fascinated by Him, but because he was called and chosen:

> You did not choose Me, but I chose you. (John 15:16)

It was by this selection that the disciples received authority and power from God to carry out the ministry (Matthew 10:1). Jesus didn't choose disciples just to prepare the Passover feast (Matthew 26:17–19), or to look for a donkey He could ride into Jerusalem (although they did both things very well, just as they were told [Matthew 21:1–6]). The disciples were His intimate friends (John 15:14) who shared in His miracles and received His teachings about this new way of life; who experienced His transfiguration (Matthew 17) and saw things that even the Prophets had wanted to see (Luke 10:23–24).

The disciples were common, ordinary people without any special preparation. Jesus was in charge of preparing them. He called them, trained them, prayed for them. He sent them out "like sheep among wolves" and asked them to be "shrewd as snakes and as innocent as doves" (Matthew 10:16).

He didn't give them a manual with instructions for any and every occasion, but rather the prudence and simplicity to discern for themselves how to act in different situations. Many times they asked Jesus childlike questions that revealed their ignorance. Other times they denied Him. Many other times they didn't understand Him and had to ask for an explanation. They had to work hard to understand Jesus' language. On one occasion, Jesus told them to watch out for the leaven of the Pharisees, and they thought He was scolding them for having forgotten to bring bread in the boat with them. Once in the boat, Jesus said to them, "How is it you don't understand that I was not talking to you about bread? But be on your guard against the yeast of the Pharisees and Sadducees" (Matthew 16:11).

Sometimes they understand neither His teachings nor the meaning of His miracles. Nor did they have the strength to accompany Him during His last moments, when Jesus asked them to pray with Him. Some of them didn't have the strength to see Him hanging from the cross. These were hard things for them. The disciples were simple human beings, full of anxieties and fears like anyone else. That's why, when Jesus recruited and sent them to preach and perform miracles, He said three times, "Do not be afraid" (Matthew 10:26, 28, 31).

But these common, ordinary people were being transformed by the company of their Teacher. One time, Jesus and His followers arrived in Caesarea Philippi where there were a number of shrines to pagan gods. People from all over had come to worship those gods. In that context, Jesus asked His disciples, "Who do people say the Son of Man is?" (Matthew 16:13). Later He asked them a much more personal question: "But what about you? . . . Who do you say I am?" (v. 15). To this question, Peter responded emphatically, "You are the Christ, the Son of the living God" (v. 16). On this declaration of the faith of one of His disciples, Jesus would build His Church.

Read Matthew 10:1–15.

What are some of the characteristics of the discipleship Jesus entrusted to the Twelve?

Part 2:
Behind the Scenes

> After the Sabbath, at dawn on the first day of the week, Mary Magdalene and the other Mary went to look at the tomb. (Matthew 28:1)

This "other Mary," who is also mentioned in Matthew 27:61, could be a symbol of all the "other disciples" of Jesus. Many of these "other disciples" don't appear by name in the Scriptures. But the Gospel writers record their acts, some formidable, some simple, but all important for establishing God's kingdom among mankind. As in a theater production, there are many who work "behind the scenes" who don't get credit for the final work but without whom it couldn't have been accomplished.

Jesus recruited more than twelve disciples, many of whom worked behind the scenes, fulfilling whatever function they were called to do. It's worth noting that while His "official disciples" (the Eleven who remained after Judas killed himself) were locked in a house because they feared the Jews, there were women who stayed in the area, "guarding" other secret disciples of Jesus when He was buried (Matthew 27:61). This faithfulness of the women following Jesus, even when He was dead, permitted them to be the first to see Him risen. The resurrection was revealed first to those who served Him quietly, and of whom little is said. It seems like the Church has forgotten Jesus' words to His disciples when Mary of Bethany anointed Him in the house of Simon the leper:

> I tell you the truth, wherever this gospel is preached throughout the world, what she

has done will also be told, in memory of her. (Matthew 26:13)

The Gospels note various Marys who were followers of Jesus. One of them was Mary of Bethany, the one who anointed Him, and of whom we should speak with greatest respect, because she prepared Jesus' body for burial. Mary could do this because, first of all, she sat at the feet of Jesus, listening to His word, enchanted, probably, because a rabbi would take the time to teach a woman in a completely patriarchal society. Mary hosted Jesus more than once since Bethany was on the way to Jerusalem. She and her sister, Martha, experienced the power and love of the Master when He raised their brother, Lazarus, from the dead (John 11).

Mary Magdalene, the first to see the risen Lord (John 20:16), was part of a group of women who financially helped Jesus and followed His preaching journeys. Mary Magdalene had experienced the healing power of Jesus in her own life (Luke 8:2), and later on became the first messenger of His resurrection. Perhaps she also experienced frustration and disappointment when the "official disciples" of Jesus didn't believe her story of Jesus' resurrection (Luke 24:11).

These Marys and other women who had followed Jesus from Galilee to Jerusalem (Matthew 27:55) belonged to a group that had seen Jesus in action, and whose lives had been completely changed by Him. Perhaps those were some of the requirements to be a disciple of Jesus. Undoubtedly, that was the experience of other secret disciples, like Nicodemus and Joseph of Arimathea. Both appeared at the just the right moment to take charge of Jesus' body when His other disciples were nowhere to be found. It was Joseph of Arimathea who asked Pilate for Jesus' body and who provided a new tomb that would be the scene of the great miracle of the resurrection. Nicodemus accompanied him, bringing seventy-five pounds of mixed myrrh with which to wrap the Lord's body.

It wasn't pity that motivated them to do these things. Neither was it the need to do a good deed. This is clear in the case of Nicodemus, a man well informed in the Jewish religion, who had known the new birth of which Jesus spoke in their first interview (John 3). The Gospels don't speak much of these secret disciples of Jesus, maybe only enough to recognize in them characteristics of true discipleship. Nicodemus was a Pharisee, and despite the fact that most Pharisees criticized Jesus secretly and openly, Nicodemus came to the Lord because he recognized Him as someone who came from God (v. 2). This is perhaps the first sign of a true disciple. Jesus confirms this with these words as He prays to His Father:

> [My disciples] knew with certainty that I came from You, and they believed that You sent Me. (John 17:8)

Nicodemus questioned Jesus, not to entrap Him like the other Pharisees did, but out of genuine interest to know more about "being born again." He defended Jesus among his peers (John 7:50–51), showing a little more courage than on the night he had come to Jesus in secret.

And there are many more mentioned by the Gospel writers only as a group of disciples whom Jesus recruited to help Him proclaim the Gospel. They worked behind the scenes, but they worked wonders. Luke says, "The seventy-two returned with joy and said, 'Lord, even the demons submit to us in Your name'" (Luke 10:17). Not only did they return rejoicing because they had been able to cast out demons, but they rejoiced that this same Jesus, full of joy in the Spirit, praised His Father because by the work of these seventy-two, He saw Satan fall from heaven like lightning (v. 18). It is interesting how Jesus reflected on their joy, saying:

> Do not rejoice that the spirits submit to you, but rejoice that your names are written in heaven. (Luke 10:20)

By that He meant that it's not about going out to fight the devil, but rather to declare the coming of the kingdom of God. Heaven is open to sinners. God, in Jesus, is walking toward them. In order to receive Him, understand Him, and be blessed by Him, the seventy-two do a work of preparation. They announce peace and judgment. These two elements always appear in Jesus' proclamation:

- Law and Gospel
- condemnation and restoration

The seventy-two disciples were sent with very specific instructions. They were selected and invested with the authority of God Himself, and they were warned that they would be "like lambs among wolves" (Luke 10:3).

Once more we see that Jesus doesn't make false promises to His disciples, and He doesn't disguise the coming of the kingdom of God with pretty words. Jesus exposes them to the reality that the work is enormous and the workers are few; that they will have to announce peace but also judgment; that they will be able to share a roof and food with a family but at other times they will have to leave a town, proclaiming condemnation. Wolves don't reject the sheep; they eat them. If the disciples were prepared to be rejected and declare judgment, they would also have to be prepared to beware of those who were ready to ambush and devour them.

There was a lot of work to do. The pressure of Satan over the people was overwhelming. There were innumerable dangers. Despite all, the seventy-two disciples returned with joy, and with all the security of having left many with joy in their hearts, anxious to know God personally so their joy would be complete. That is, after all is said and done, the function of a disciple is to announce that the kingdom of God is very near—*very near*—in Jesus, and that true joy is only found in Him.

Read Luke 10:1–12.

Discover some of the characteristics of discipleship according to the mission that Jesus entrusted to the seventy-two.

Part 3:
Jesus Calls Me to a Ministry of Joy

I am as much a disciple as any other believer in Christ. I was called to a ministry of joy, to rejoice in the Holy Spirit just like the first disciples Jesus recruited. Spiritual joy is one of the distinguishing characteristics of Jesus' followers, whether they are on the front lines or behind the scenes. Sometimes, for various reasons, I compare myself to those first disciples Jesus called. Sometimes, because I am so overcome by weariness, I fall asleep, just like the disciples that night in Gethsemane while Jesus was in agony. I recognize in myself Jesus' assertion that "the spirit is willing, but the body is weak" (Matthew 26:41). That is exactly what I recognize—that as a disciple, I have good intentions and a spirit that is ready, but I lack strength and fall asleep, leaving Jesus to work alone.

It's possible that this happens to me because I want to do more than one disciple should do. The call of Jesus to Simon and Andrew was:

> Come, follow Me . . . and I will make you fishers of men. (Matthew 4:19)

This is also how God calls each of His followers, to be fishermen. But besides fishing, we also want to clean the fish and leave them "our kind of clean" in the kingdom of God. Someone said once that "we fish and God cleans." Cleaning sinners is God's job, not ours. That's why He died on the cross and rose victorious.

Other times, I compare myself to the twelve disciples because I don't understand the teachings of Jesus and have to ask questions, to go time and time again to the

Scriptures to spend time alone with my Teacher and His Word in order to understand His teaching.

I am often like those who were behind the scenes. Without being seen by anyone, I work in support of those who are at the front of the battle. I testify, I give my time and my money, I accompany, I share, I hold, and I listen. I enjoy the company of those who are with me behind the scenes. Their enthusiasm and dedication encourage me, and I rejoice in the gifts that God has given them and in the way they put them to use for the great fishing.

Sometimes my "flesh is weak" in different ways. I don't have much patience with new disciples. I forget that there must be a time of formation while one begins to walk with Jesus. The Lord invested years to develop His disciples. He didn't give them an intensive course for a few weeks. He worked with them day and night, on dry land and walking on the water. He made them witness the most spectacular miracles and acts of love never seen before. He made them listen to the true interpretation of the Law; He taught them to pray, to not be afraid, and to see life through a totally different lens. Above all, "beginning with Moses and all the Prophets, He explained to them what was said in all the Scriptures concerning Himself" (Luke 24:27). This reminds me that I am a disciple in formation and that I still have to walk a long way behind Jesus in order to listen attentively to His Word and follow His example.

Another weakness of mine is that it's hard for me to let go of everything I have in my hands so I can put them fully on the plow. And when I place my hands on the plow, I don't always look straight ahead. I get distracted. There are so many things in this world! And so many seem indispensable! I always remember the humor of a South American entertainer who, referring to our consumer society, said: "When I go to the supermarket, I like to look at all the things I don't need!" It's true. I don't need all the things that consumerism puts in front of me as indispensable. "Only one thing is needed," Jesus told Martha in Bethany while He taught her and her sister, Mary. Listening to God's message is the one thing that is needed. The apostle Matthew reaffirms this truth for me when he records Jesus' words in the Sermon on the Mount:

> But seek first His kingdom and His righteousness, and all these things will be given to you as well. (Matthew 6:33)

It was not in vain that Jesus sent out the seventy-two disciples, telling them, "Do not take a purse or bag or sandals; and do not greet anyone on the road" (Luke 10:4). These words from the Lord reaffirm in me the certainty that He will provide all I need to be an effective disciple.

One thing that gets my attention about discipleship is the figurative language Jesus uses, more specifically, the mention of different kinds of animals to refer to both the disciples and the people to be made disciples: serpents, scorpions, doves, lambs, wolves. The serpents and scorpions represent enemy powers over which God gives me authority to trample underfoot. There are scorpions and serpents out there that are crouching, ready to spring. They are people full of venom who wound and hurt whoever crosses their path. They're everywhere, and their names are called Pornography, Evolutionism, Terrorism, Tarot, and Spiritualism, among many others. We need to understand that Jesus' authority over these venomous enemies is not to avoid them, but to stamp them out, to keep them from doing their damage. What work for the disciple of the Lord! That is why Jesus warned the seventy-two disciples before sending them out:

> The harvest is plentiful, but the workers are few. Ask the Lord of the harvest, therefore, to send out workers into His harvest field. (Luke 10:2)

And those who are not serpents and scorpions are wolves that can devastate and devour the Lord's lambs. That is why we should not be distressed. We must be attentive, keeping our hands on the plow and our eyes firmly fixed ahead on the goal Jesus puts before us. The serpents, scorpions, and wolves don't turn away from their goal, which is to destroy the Lord's lambs. Being innocent as doves doesn't mean we should be gullible and naïve.

But all is not danger and weakness. We need to remember that, despite our own insufficiency and the forces of the enemy that surround us, we were called to a ministry of joy. The seventy-two disciples returned filled with joy, and even Jesus rejoiced with them in the Spirit, bursting into praise to the Father (Luke 10:17, 21).

Above all, I enjoy the great benefit of having been caught and cleaned by Jesus Himself. Only He could clean me completely and change me into a person innocent as a dove and docile as a lamb. Without His forgiveness, I would be a wolf and a scorpion, just like any other malicious force. He changed me completely. He chose me as He chose the Twelve, as He chose the seventy-two, and as He chose so many others behind the scenes.

Since that moment, following Jesus has been an adventure for me. I never know where He will call me or what future ministry He is preparing for me. I do know that it is fascinating, because Jesus always surprises me, either when I find Him in the Scriptures or when He produces fruits through me that I never could have imagined.

Read Acts 8:4–8 and 13:49–52.

Think about the characteristics of the ministry among the first evangelists of the Church. Pay special attention to the joy felt by those who announced the Good News and those who received it.

Chapter 9

Part 1:
The Ministry of Jesus: Preaching and Miracles

Jesus didn't waste any time. Immediately after His Baptism, He began His public ministry. He came into the world with a well-defined purpose and committed Himself to finish it without interruptions.

- What was His ministry?
- What were its characteristics?

There are many answers. Even the evangelists record Jesus' activities in four different ways. Therefore, it would be difficult to define Jesus' public ministry in just a few words because a number of important characteristics would be left out. Let us reflect on the way Jesus Himself defined His activity on earth.

He summed up the characteristics of His ministry with these words:

> The Son of Man did not come to be served, but to serve, and to give His life as a ransom for many. (Matthew 20:28)

Although He never forgot the final goal of dying in the place of sinners to rescue them from temporary and eternal condemnation, Jesus developed a ministry of compassion and warning.

He first preached in the synagogues, and when things became complicated in the central meeting places of the Jews, He went out to preach in the towns of Israel, accompanied by His disciples, whom He instructed along the way. He recognized in His contemporaries the profound need for spiritual peace, emotional health, healthy relationships, and freedom from sicknesses. This is why His ministry of compassion included promises like this one:

> Come to Me, all you who are weary and burdened, and I will give you rest. (Matthew 11:28)

He included different kinds of warnings:

> Enter through the narrow gate. For wide is the gate . . . that leads to destruction, and many enter through it. (Matthew 7:13)

> Watch out for false prophets. . . . Inwardly they are ferocious wolves. (Matthew 7:15)

> Not everyone who says to Me, 'Lord, Lord,' will enter the kingdom of heaven, but only he who does the will of My Father who is in heaven. (Matthew 7:21)

He included miracles of health, curing all kinds of diseases, lepers, the handicapped, the blind, the deaf and mute, the lame, and even the resurrection of the dead (Matthew 8:16).

During His ministry, Jesus tried to do good, not to get attention or to become popular, but because doing good was an inherent part of His personality. Wherever Jesus went, things changed radically. The miracles He performed were the natural result of who He was. He just couldn't work any other way!

Many people, including the religious leaders, didn't understand Jesus' ministry, His miracles, and His compassion. They accused Him of being satanic, of performing miracles by the power of Satan. Others didn't understand His ministry because they were not accustomed to seeing such a display of authority, power, and love. And still others didn't understand because they didn't know what to expect of the promised Messiah. An example could be John the Baptist, who sent his disciples, while he was in jail, to ask Jesus if He was the Messiah. Jesus responded:

> Go back and report to John what you hear and see: The blind receive sight, the lame walk, those who have leprosy are cured, the deaf hear, the dead are raised, and the good news is preached to the poor. (Matthew 11:4–5)

That is exactly what can be expected from the true Messiah sent by God.

The problem that confounded so many about the ministry of Jesus is that the characteristics of His work had not been seen before and were different from what people were used to. Jesus spent time with people of questionable reputation; He was not troubled by contact with Gentiles, He didn't belong to a reclusive sect in the desert, and

He didn't lead an ascetic hermit life. On the contrary, He didn't let the wine run out at weddings where He was invited (John 2). He didn't bind Himself to strict rituals as the religious leaders and any person considered a faithful follower of the Law were used to doing. Jesus specifically declared that for Him and for His Father, people were more important than any religious laws. When Jesus' enemies tried to trick Him, they asked:

> "Is it lawful to heal on the Sabbath?" He said to them, "If any of you has a sheep and it falls into a pit on the Sabbath, will you not take hold of it and lift it out? How much more valuable is a man than a sheep! Therefore it is lawful to do good on the Sabbath." (Matthew 12:10–12)

On one occasion, Jesus explained through a parable that His teaching and action didn't fit into the traditional molds. "The new wine of the Gospel cannot be stored in old wineskins," Jesus was saying, trying to open the minds of those who debated Him and even His own disciples, so they might recognize that God's way of working cannot be adjusted to the limits imposed by traditions, fears, and even institutionalized religion. In the same parable, Jesus affirmed that He didn't come to fix a situation, but to renovate it completely.

It's right to say His ministry was complete. Jesus moved with total freedom. He performed miracles however and wherever He wanted, some of them "programmed," as when He deliberately waited until Lazarus died so that later He could raise him from the dead with power (John 11); other miracles were spontaneous, such as the resurrection of the son of the widow of Nain (Luke 7:11–17). Some of His miracles and teachings were done in private, intimately (Matthew 9:18–31) and others were open to all the public

(Matthew 5:1; Mark 4:34). But perhaps seeing Jesus in action was the best way to understand the diversity and depth of His ministry.

The Gospel writers describe with detail a series of events that happened in just a matter of hours. Jesus, seated in a boat, taught the crowds that gathered on the shore, and later, in a more intimate atmosphere, He explained these teachings to His disciples.

That same day, at nightfall, He invited them to go to the other side of the lake, to an area of Greek cities where the inhabitants spoke more than one language and practiced more than one religion. For the Jews, the "other side" was an unclean place, populated by people who practiced a different culture, unacceptable to the people of Israel. This invitation from Jesus, to step outside the limits of the clean area, would have produced some discomfort among His disciples. Moments later, discomfort gave place to fear, because a storm battered them and their boat was sinking.

Although Jesus calmed the storm and left His disciples with mouths wide open in astonishment, when they landed, things got difficult. A man with a terrible, frightening appearance approached them; he was filled with demons, was untamable, and had lived among graves, the unclean places. The demons asked Jesus to leave them in peace. Then, two thousand pigs showed up ***and Jesus gave the demons permission to enter the pigs***. Pigs are unclean animals to the Jews, and the two thousand of them made a great commotion in the lake, drowning, contaminating the waters, and making the herdsmen run away, terrified.

Jesus' impact in this "other place" was such that the people asked Him to leave that place. They couldn't bear changes in their lives. The man healed by Jesus was the only one who was content; and he was not only content, but so energized by God that Mark ends his account (Mark 4–5:20) by saying, "So the man went away and began to tell in the Decapolis how much Jesus had done for him. And all the people were amazed" (Mark 5:20).

Among the exhaustion of the disciples, the fears, the storms, the demon-possessed, the unclean places, the pigs, and the rejection of the people shines the last moment of Jesus' journey, which is summarized in the words He said to the demon-possessed man:

> Go home to your family and tell them how much the Lord has done for you, and how He has had mercy on you. (Mark 5:19)

Read Mark 4–5:20.

List at least four outstanding aspects of the events related in this passage.

Part 2:
Binding Satan

The apostle and Gospel writer John, who was eyewitness to the ministry of Jesus, categorically affirms:

> The reason the Son of God appeared was to destroy the devil's work. (1 John 3:8)

The devil's works are evil and many. In this same passage, John observes that the devil sinned from the beginning. From the time he tempted Adam and Eve to disobey God, Satan has done nothing but attack and destroy God's creation. Jesus says very clearly that the devil "was a murderer from the beginning, not holding to the truth, for there is no truth in him" (John 8:44).

The devil is the number one enemy of God and His creation, so the forgiveness of sins wouldn't do any good if the source and origin of evil are not destroyed. But there is a process for everything. Jesus didn't come to annihilate Satan, to make him disappear from the scene in order to radically change the world. Jesus came not to destroy Satan, but to destroy his works. The fire is prepared for the devil and all of his angels (Matthew 25:41), Jesus said, and Satan's days are numbered. Actually, all his days are numbered since God warned the serpent in the Garden of Eden that from that moment on there would be a permanent enmity between humanity and Satan; and that in a given moment in history, the Descendant of the woman would crush the devil's head (Genesis 3:15).

The incarnation of God in a human body was the final sentence for Satan. That is why Satan so forcefully pursued Jesus in so many different ways: killing the baby boys of Bethlehem by Herod's hand after Jesus' birth (Matthew 2:16), tempting Him to practice His ministry with a different spirit (4:1–11), and even accusing Him of being in league with Satan himself (12:24). That is why the Gospel writers tell so many stories of demon-possessed people being healed during Jesus' ministry. It is interesting to observe the biblical language used to describe these miracles: "The demon was driven out" (Matthew 9:33) is a clear reference to the fact that with His arrival, "the prince of this world will be driven out" (John 12:31). Knowing this situation, Jesus admits that part of His ministry is to bind Satan. Thus He explains to the Jews who had accused Him of being demoniac:

> If I drive out demons by the Spirit of God, then the kingdom of God has come upon you. Or again, how can anyone enter a strong man's house and carry off his possessions unless he first ties up the strong man? Then he can rob his house. (Matthew 12:28–29)

Jesus knew that He, as the incarnation of God, assumed human nature. He was the descendant of Eve who was charged with crushing the devil's head. The object was to let the devil be still for a moment and then strike the blow to his head. If He didn't bind him first, He might crush his tail or part of his body, and that was not God's plan. The devil needed to be left blind and with his head crushed under the powerful, divine foot to stop him from biting and poisoning God's creation the way he had done centuries before.

But binding Satan was not easy. The Bible describes him from the beginning as a snake. It is a very powerful symbol for many reasons. Snakes come in different shapes and colors, and they range from harmless to mortally dangerous. It is notable that even nonpoisonous snakes cause panic and terror among people. With rare exceptions, people don't want to have anything to do with snakes. Snakes generally move along the ground, easily hidden among rocks and vegetation, waiting to spring on their victims, to attack them when they least expect it. In extreme cases, snakes can kill a victim in a matter of minutes. God once used poisonous snakes to teach a lesson to the people of Israel. After they left Egypt under the hands of Moses, the people of Israel became discouraged while they were in the desert and began to murmur against God. God sent snakes that bit them, "and many Israelites died" (Numbers 21:6). It remained this way until the people recognized their fault and asked Moses, "Pray that the LORD will take the snakes away from us" (v. 7).

This event is a strong symbol of the events of human history. We are poisoned by Satan. We murmur against God when we find ourselves in deserts of opposition and when we don't want a leader to direct us. The devil's poison is so potent that it takes us directly to death. Only God can take the snakes away!

This image was very clear in Jesus' mind when He began to bind Satan in order to stop him and crush his head. Love for God's creation carried the Messiah forward to face God's number one enemy with determination. And binding the devil is a complicated task. He doesn't have a neck that can be roped or hands or feet that can be shackled. He is too slippery, silent, and crafty. How can he be bound? How can he be restrained in order to give him a hard blow on the head and take him out of the fight? By destroying his works, cleansing the demon-possessed, and refuting the children of the devil personified in some of the Jews and Pharisees (John 8:44).

John the Baptist and Jesus referred to the Pharisees as "snakes" and "vipers" (Matthew 3:7; 23:33). These people will not be able to escape the condemnation of hell unless they recognize that they are infected with deadly poison. Denouncing the hypocrisy and false religion of Israel's religious leaders, Jesus binds the devil, undoes his work, and leaves him without weapons, because Satan's weapon is the lie, and Jesus came to bring the truth (John 8:44–45). In this way, Jesus held him still and brought all the weight of His divinity to bear on his head. From the cross, nailed hand and foot, impossible to move physically, Jesus stretched His foot of justice and, with a well-aimed blow, He left Satan's head immobilized. "It is finished!" He cried before dying, successfully culminating another part of His ministry of salvation for humanity. The warning of Genesis 3:15 had been fulfilled. The devil was out of the fight.

Jesus' victory over the main enemy of God and His creation will be consummated on the final Judgment Day. Meanwhile, the devil continues to do harm. Although his head is crushed, his tail is loose, and his body can make many trip and fall.

It is a great comfort for the redeemed to know that Jesus has been victorious in His attempt to bind Satan. Seeing Jesus in action—facing satanic accusations, confronting the demon-possessed who called out for internal peace, and even facing frontal attacks of the devil during His time of prayer and fasting before beginning His ministry—brings great relief and peace. It is important to know that the King of this world has thrown down the satanic prince of this world. Satan no longer has power over the children of God.

Read Matthew 12:22–29.

How does the coming of the kingdom of God relate to Jesus casting out demons?

Read John 8:42–47.

What arguments does Jesus use to tell the Jews they are children of the devil?

Part 3:
The Harvest Is Plentiful

"Go and make disciples of all nations" (Matthew 28:19), Jesus said to His followers before leaving this world. "Go and make disciples of all nations." I have read this passage many times. I have heard it in church every year since I was a child. I have seen it written on postcards and posters and framed on the wall in Christian homes. I have sung its words to many different melodies. I have listened to preaching on this theme in many evangelism and mission services. I myself have even preached on these words of Jesus a number of times and to different audiences. It is the easiest passage to find in the Bible. But it wasn't until recently that I discovered the depth of God's universal love and the complexity that the Church faces to fulfill this Great Commission. It was just a few years ago that I understood that in order to make disciples of all nations, I had to step to the "other side."

The word "nations" used in Matthew is the translation of the Greek term *ethne*. From *ethne* we get the English word *ethnic*. So we can translate the Great Commission as follows: "Go and make disciples of all ethnicities." Now our passage has a broader meaning. I understand better why Jesus didn't minister only to the Jews. He came as Savior of the whole world, not just one chosen ethnic group.

God's love is universal:

> For God does not show favoritism.
> (Romans 2:11)

God loves everyone the same. I understand the challenges that face the Church when it tries to be faithful to this Great Commission. It is necessary to go to the "other side," to pass through storms, to meet people who are different from us, who don't speak the same language, and who, of course, don't worship the same god. They are different and are submerged in a culture that we don't understand and many times don't even like.

Going to the "other side" generally means entering an unknown territory, and the unknown usually produces fear. That's why many churches are not multiethnic. It isn't because they haven't read the Great Commission, but because they feel uncomfortable entering the unknown world of the "other side." God knows our fears and insecurities, which is why Jesus added these words:

> I am with you always, to the very end of the age. (Matthew 28:20)

Personally, I have often invented excuses for not crossing over to the other side. I saw too many storms and "demon-possessed" who came out to meet me. I saw people who didn't speak my language; who didn't sing the same hymns; who didn't have a routine, a liturgy for prayer and worship. Such different people!

There were other passages of Scripture that God used to make me see His universal love so that my ministry also would have a universal or multiethnic reach. When the people of Israel left Egypt under the command of Moses, the Scriptures state that "many other people went up with them" (Exodus 12:38). God used the opportunity to liberate other ethnic groups and take them out as a whole to a land of freedom. God is inclusive. What a great contrast with my attitude of liking to be exclusive! I didn't like to associate with just anybody—especially if they didn't share my values, my culture, or my way of doing things. But God, who does not exclude any group, had patience with me, enlightened me, and called me to go with Him to the "other side." He made me pass through storms, fears, and embarrassments until I learned to enrich myself with other ethnic groups, and He surprised me with how many gifts He had given to those who were not like me.

Those groups enriched me with their music, their values and traditions, and their enthusiasm and passion for the Gospel that encourages me today to serve in my ministry with more joy. "The harvest is plentiful, but the workers are few" (Luke 10:2), both on "this side" and on the "other side." There's more than enough work in the Lord's fields! Sometimes that's what makes me want to do more than what God has planned for me to do. It's just that we're so few! I forget that Jesus didn't get overrun by trying to do everything all at once, nor did He do it alone. If He had tried to satisfy all the immediate needs of the people, He would not have had time to go to the cross and die for the people of all the nations. He would still be in Galilee, healing the sick and denouncing the hypocritical Pharisees. It's a good thing God didn't lose sight of the ultimate end of His ministry. What a lesson for me and for the whole Church!

We recognize that the harvest is plentiful and we get ahead of ourselves, ministering to them without taking the time to study their culture, to learn what they need, and to learn their language. We answer questions before they have been fully formed. We don't take the time to listen to people and hear about their fears and insecurities. So we try to harvest before the field is ripe, or sometimes even before the seed of the Word has taken root.

I have also observed that one of the great challenges is within the same institutionalized Church, so stuck in its traditions, to their things from "this side," the comfort of the known. Since its birth, the institutionalized Church has served immigrant people as a way of helping them preserve their cultural characteristics and their values. It's no wonder that the first conflict in the Early Church began when those in charge of social ministry didn't give equal attention to everyone. Luke says, "The Grecian Jews among them complained against the Hebraic Jews because their widows were being overlooked in the daily distribution of food" (Acts 6:1). The solution was to put more people to work, or better yet, to distribute the work among a greater number of workers.

The workers are few, and among the few, we have limitations. Or perhaps we look too much at our limitations and too little at Jesus' promise: "I am with you always, to the very end of age" (Matthew 28:20). His promise is not limited by time, space, or power. It doesn't matter where I'm called to develop my work; He will be there with me, as He has always been with His Church, and as He will be to the end of time. I am convinced that I have to look less at my limitations and more to Jesus, His ministry, and His promises. Today He's still right: the harvest is plentiful . . . both on "this side" and the "other side." He's not only still right, but He still has the power to encourage me, and the whole Church, to approach people of different ethnic groups without fear. He still has the power to help me discover the best channels to communicate His love in many and different ways. He still has the power to calm the storms that frighten me and to fill me with the joy of the Holy Spirit each time, by my testimony, God rescues one more sinner.

Read Matthew 28:19–21.

Analyze the passage and reflect on some new aspect that you have learned today.

Chapter 10

Part 1: *Jesus' Ministry in "Living Color"*

The popularity Jesus gained in just three years of ministry was incredible. We need to understand that He didn't try to be popular. Several times, after a miracle, He warned, "See that you don't tell anyone" (Matthew 8:4). He even avoided going to Jerusalem, where doctors of the Law and other religious leaders waited to confront Him and challenge His new teachings. It would have been easy for Jesus to demolish them with His divine wisdom and win the favor of many. How easy it would have been to take advantage of His power to do miracles, leaving the whole world happy and satisfied, and thus gain supporters for His cause.

But Jesus didn't do any of that. He was popular because His works and teachings made an impact on people's hearts. He was also popular because He came to a people who were almost desperate, drowning in political anxiety and social and cultural deterioration. Jesus could be the one to restore the nation! But He wanted to restore all nations, not just one. That's why He went to Jerusalem.

Along with Him went people who had seen and heard firsthand of the resurrection of Lazarus (John 11). Others knew the blind man Bartimaeus, whose sight Jesus had recently restored near Jericho (Mark 10:46–52).

Two groups of people filled with excitement and happiness were found near Jerusalem. They cut down branches and placed them on the road where Jesus would pass. They took their cloaks and placed them down so the donkey carrying Jesus could walk over them. Everyone wanted to take part in this event. "Save us now! Please, save us now!" they shouted. The Galileans who came with Jesus and the rest of the disciples were proud to go to the temple for the Passover feast, accompanied by a true prophet who raised the dead and gave sight to the blind.

It's notable that "when Jesus entered Jerusalem, the whole city was stirred" (Matthew 21:10). This is the second time that the entire city was shaken because of Jesus. The first time was when the Wise Men from the East passed through Jerusalem to ask about the newborn King of the Jews. This second time, it was the entrance of that King who came to die in just a few days. But most of the crowd didn't know about His imminent death. They were too downhearted under Herod and the Roman governors. Jesus would make a magnificent king. Without launching any kind of campaign, crowds followed Him and the whole city was shaken. How could they be made to understand the true meaning of Jesus' kingdom? How could they be made to see that life is more than self-centered nationalism?

Jesus expressed Himself clearly when He said, "My kingdom is not of this world" (John 18:36). For years He'd preached that the kingdom of God was near, that it would be difficult for the rich to enter this kingdom, and that His people should pray that God's kingdom might come. Now the King presented Himself, but not by riding on a horse under strict security measures and accompanied by a military escort. Instead of a triumphal entrance, this seemed more like an impromptu parade.

These are the last days of Jesus' earthly life and the events they precipitated. But nothing happened by chance. The context in which these events occurred was special. It was less than a week before the great Passover celebration. Many sincere Jews were preparing to commemorate this religious feast with all the appropriate solemnity and passion. Many families in Jerusalem and the surrounding areas were preparing to receive family and friends who were coming from all parts of the world. Those who supplied the temple with animals for the sacrifices hoped business would be good. The Romans looked on with a sharp eye and redoubled their security. They knew that the festivals in Jerusalem were ripe for popular uprisings. Herod occupied his place as king, not chosen by but imposed on the people. The religious leaders were on the hunt for heretics and unauthorized teachers. Feverish activity was unfolding throughout Jerusalem.

A donkey was there, just as Zechariah had prophesied hundreds of years earlier (Zechariah 9:9). And there were young people praising God, as had also been prophesied by David:

> From the lips of children and infants You have ordained praise because of Your enemies. (Psalm 8:2)

There was no lack of enemies. God provided praise for Jesus from the most innocent and the least understood—or better said, from the ones who didn't analyze things.

On the road between Bethany and Jerusalem, there was also that fig tree with leaves but no fruit. The tree was unusual because it was not the season for figs. When a fig tree has leaves, it's supposed to have figs. Jesus got up early and left for Bethany to continue His ministry in Jerusalem. He was hungry and approached the fig tree that pretended to be something it was not. Disappointed, Jesus cursed it: " 'May you never bear fruit again!' Immediately the tree withered" (Matthew 21:19). The disciples were there with Him, and they never ceased to be amazed by what Jesus said and did. "How did the fig tree wither so quickly?" they asked, amazed (v. 20). Had the disciples understood that Jesus had just taught one of His more eloquent parables? The fig tree was the people of Israel getting ready for the feast. There was a lot of activity in the temple: buying and selling, exchanging money. There are plenty of leaves but no fruit. No fruit! God would make Israel wither completely because it didn't offer what it was supposed to offer: fruit! God was hungry for fruit. When He looks for fruit among His people, He expects to find it. He doesn't want to see just leaves. The Pharisees had made the people of Israel accustomed to producing leaves rather than fruit.

When an interpreter of the Law approached Jesus to tempt Him by asking which commandment was the most important, he had to recognize, when confronted with Jesus' answer, that loving God and your neighbor "is more important than all burnt offerings and sacrifices" (Mark 12:33). Burnt offerings and sacrifices are foliage. Loving God "with all your heart, with all your understanding and with all your strength, and to love your neighbor as yourself" (v. 33) are the fruits. The interpreter of the Law knew it clearly, but he didn't put it into practice, which is why Jesus said, "You are not far from the kingdom of God" (v. 34).

Jesus entered Jerusalem as a King, bringing with Him an invisible kingdom. He entered Jerusalem in a humble way, riding on a donkey, enjoying the praises of the little children, and hoping that many might be able to understand His ministry. God brings a kingdom in Jesus so the people might be in Him, not just near Him. It's no use to be "not far from the kingdom of God." We must be *in* it. Jesus entered Jerusalem so His people might reign together with Him forever, from the inside.

Read Matthew 21:1–11.

Describe the qualities of Jesus that are found in this event.

Part 2:
Jesus Expresses His Deepest Feelings

From the Mount of Olives from which Jesus came as He approached Jerusalem, you can get a view of almost the entire city. The Mount of Olives is even higher than the hill on which Jerusalem is built, so you can see what's happening on the temple porches. That is what you see first: the temple. So many emotions, memories, and hopes gathered in the heart of the Jew when he saw the temple while coming down the mountainside. Jesus was no exception.

In contrast, notice:

- On one hand, the people are festive. It's almost Passover. Family and friends are arriving, and many people have been encouraged and cheered by Jesus' miracles.
- On the other hand, Jesus stops and weeps for the city. He agonizes over it. He can see that its people are wearing a blindfold that keeps them from seeing God's love.

> If you, even you, had only known on this day what would bring you peace—but now it is hidden from your eyes. (Luke 19:42)

Jesus is deeply moved for the thousands of people who are celebrating but don't understand God. They live in deceit. He has come to free them from their error but they don't believe Him. Jesus already knows it will be this way, which makes His ministry even more incredible. He doesn't abandon everything. He doesn't say, "It isn't worth the trouble. They're all blind." Neither does He become desperate and put into action a plan to evangelize the city by force. Jesus weeps. He lets go of His emotions in front of the people. The Gospel writer Luke noted all the details of that moment. Jesus not only saw the feverish activity in Jerusalem and its surroundings, but He also saw what would happen to all those formidable buildings of which the disciples were so proud. Everything was going to be destroyed. Not a single one of those fantastic foundations would remain where the builders had placed them with so much effort.

Several years later, the Romans besieged and destroyed the city completely, including the temple, the great national symbol and distinctive monument of the people of Israel. Jesus saw how Daniel's prophecy would be fulfilled:

> The Anointed One will be cut off and will have nothing. The people of the ruler who will come will destroy the city and the sanctuary. (Daniel 9:26)

Jesus' anguish can be understood because, in His ability to see the future, He could perceive the suffering of the people during those times. Not only did Jesus carry all the sins of the people, He also took their sufferings, both past and future. Great suffering would come in future days. So He saw and so He said:

> How dreadful it will be in those days for pregnant women and nursing mothers! (Matthew 24:19)

Jesus advises His listeners that when those times come, they should flee to the mountains without wasting any time, and they should pray that those turbulent days might not be so terrible.

Jesus doesn't weep because Israel's identity will be destroyed with the horrible sacrilege of the temple, but for the pain His children will suffer, those He came to rescue. He weeps because Israel doesn't recognize the day of her salvation. It's one thing to not have hope, peace, or salvation. It's another thing to have them all within your reach, free for the taking, and not recognize it.

Jesus weeps because He notices the people of the city are so wrapped up in the feast that they don't even pay attention to what God is bringing them. Behind the people's happy exterior hides their uncertainty and lack of peace.

Many people knew this. There were unscrupulous people in Israel who didn't hesitate to take advantage of people who were feeling guilty, the ones who carried unforgiven sins on their shoulders, and those who were afraid of the coming punishment because they knew their lives were not exactly the best examples of sincerity and honesty.

These people went to the temple and bought sheep and doves at exorbitant prices for their sacrifices. Many probably believed that it was worth spending a small fortune to have their sins taken away. The unscrupulous ones knew this. They knew the people, especially foreigners, would not bring a sheep from home, so they raised the price of their merchandise. The sellers and money changers took advantage of the weight of the people's sin in order to get rich. They played with the most intimate feelings of their people.

When Jesus saw that this was happening, He became furious as never seen before in His ministry. The Gospel writer John paints a dramatic picture when he describes the scene:

> [Jesus] made a whip out of cords, and drove all from the temple area, both sheep and cattle; He scattered the coins of the money changers and overturned their tables. (John 2:15)

Cattle are big, heavy animals. Sheep can be noisy when they are hurried. The money changers would have cursed loudly while scrambling to pick up their scattered coins from the floor. Who is this? "By what authority are You doing these things? . . . Who gave You this authority?" (Matthew 21:23). The chief priests and the elders of the people questioned Jesus this way because they had never seen anything like this before.

It is strange to see Jesus so angry when just moments before He expressed His deepest sensitivity and compassion as He wept for the blindness of His city. Anger is the holy attitude of God when He is faced with sin. Jesus didn't think twice. It was clear: the house of His Father was a house of prayer, nothing else, and although it was soon to be destroyed, in the meantime it should serve as the place where the children of God could go to be peaceful and concentrate on their prayers.

Where did Jesus get this idea? From Scripture:

> These I will bring to My holy mountain and give them joy in My house of prayer. (Isaiah 56:7)

There was nothing wrong with offering sacrifices to God in the temple, nor was anything wrong with purchasing animals for those sacrifices. The bad thing about it was the abuse, the exchange of true inner repentance for exterior worship. All this formed part of what the Gospel writer Mark says about Jesus in that situation:

> Jesus entered Jerusalem and went to the temple. He looked around at everything . . . [and] He went out to Bethany with the Twelve. (Mark 11:11)

Jesus looked at everything, even the hearts of the people. He saw all who were under the heavy weight of sin, as well as the abusers and indifferent people. He saw those who wanted to see their nation liberated as well as those who came to lay a trap for Him with trick questions. He also saw those who suffered physical illnesses:

> The blind and the lame came to Him at the temple, and He healed them. (Matthew 21:14)

Jesus was very moved by this, so He went into action. That was a constant in His ministry. Nothing went unnoticed by His eyes.

During this last week of His life, Jesus can be seen demonstrating His passion for the people and His zeal for the things of God. Jesus takes these things very seriously, to the point that He voluntarily lays down His life so that the people's situation can be radically changed. He wants the spiritually blind to be able to see, and those who are crippled by the weight of their burdens to be able to walk upright. Jesus came to place the kingdom of God in the midst of His people. It is a magnificent kingdom where Jesus Himself reigns in love, forgiving and healing and putting hope and peace in the hearts of His children.

Read Luke 19:11–44.

Analyze Jesus' compassionate attitude.

Describe other qualities of Jesus that are brought out in this text.

Part 3:
Jesus, My King

I don't remember the day Jesus came into my life, nor do I remember when He brought me into His kingdom. All I know is that when they baptized me, Jesus cleansed the temple of my person. By His own sacrifice on the cross as the Lamb of God, He forgave my sins, healed my spiritual blindness, and prepared me to walk upright through this life with head held high, as one who has God Himself for his Father, and the very same only-begotten Son of God as the only King and Lord of his life.

How can I not walk with head held high now that God has given me the privilege of belonging to His eternal kingdom? The kingdom of heaven is very special and different from those we usually see. First of all, we don't need to change kings every so often, because King Jesus never dies. His heavenly Father crowned Him forever. There's no danger of anyone usurping His throne. That makes me feel good, secure, protected, and directed. Of course, I am not alone. In this kingdom, all of us that were washed by the blood of the Lamb are together. It's what we have in common, what unites us, and what makes us gather week after week to go to the temple and shout, "Save us now! Please, save us! Blessed is He who comes in the name of the Lord!"

Seeing the faith and passion of other members of the kingdom encourages me. Praising God together and celebrating His entry into our lives gives me joy. I feel ashamed when the cold, hard stones shout for joy because I don't.

Belonging to Jesus' kingdom has its privileges. It is a kingdom where there is crying, as when King Jesus wept for those who didn't see the goodness of God. I weep inside when I see how many people go through this life without knowing the Father's love.

It is a kingdom under attack, generally by "those who are not far" from God's kingdom, but who are not a part of it. They are the Pharisees of our time. They want Christians to have plenty of leaves, but little or no fruit. They want us to stay busy with activities that distract us from the real fruit.

It is a kingdom where absolute obedience to God is demanded:

> You shall have no other gods before Me. (Exodus 20:3)

It is a kingdom where we need to love our neighbor as ourselves (Matthew 22:39).

It is a kingdom where mistakes are accepted, where you forgive others and yourself for not measuring up to what God asks of us in His commandments.

It is a kingdom where a banquet is constantly celebrated. The table is set. Every Sunday, every Christian feast day, the new Passover is celebrated with King Jesus present. He provides the proper clothes for the feast, white as snow, so I can enter into His presence pure, immaculate, and without a single wrinkle or crease. In this banquet where only bread and wine are served, God gives me His own Son, in body and blood, so I can delight in His forgiveness and be strengthened in my faith. I like to share Holy Communion with my wife and children and with many brothers and sisters of different cultures and nationalities.

Jesus' kingdom unites us and erases bitter differences, highlighting the gifts the King gives to His people. It is true that we don't always see the gifts of others. Sometimes we only want our own gifts to be seen, but God forgives us of this too.

It is a kingdom where God cures our blindness and our selfish attitude of not seeing the needs around us so that the saying "There is no greater blindness than that which doesn't want to see" is not spoken about us. I knew somebody who had serious vision problems, but in faith he could say, "Now that I can't see well, God is teaching me to see with my heart." King Jesus amplifies our sight so we can see beyond what our eyes see.

One of the things that impresses me most about this last week of Jesus' life and His ministry in Jerusalem is the purification of the temple. This is what I see: Don't play with the things of God. It is obvious that it isn't a question of living religion the way one thinks it should be but how God establishes it.

From inside Jesus' kingdom, everything has a different perspective. You can see things such as when Jesus entered the city and went to the temple to observe everything. Perhaps the saddest thing I observed was how easily everything was degraded. God established a place of prayer, and His own people turned it into a den of robbers. I have been in many basilicas and great churches where unscrupulous people sell holy cards and statues, candles and all kinds of religious charms, and where many who are "not far from the kingdom" are deceived and don't examine their hearts or look to King Jesus.

The popular religious movements don't see the crucified and resurrected Jesus from the Scriptures. They follow the dictates of their own blinded spirits. In fact, many follow the paths of "respectable religious leaders." A scene comes to mind where Jesus lays bare the teachings of the Pharisees right in front of their noses, and in front of the people says:

> You hypocrites! Isaiah was right when he prophesied about you: "These people honor Me with their lips, but their hearts are far from Me." . . . Then the disciples came to Him and asked, "Do You know that the Pharisees were offended when they heard this?" He replied, "Every plant that My heavenly Father has not planted will be pulled up by the roots. Leave them; they are blind guides. If a blind man leads a blind man, both will fall into a pit." (Matthew 15:7–8, 12–14)

I wouldn't want to be in the Pharisees' shoes when the Lord comes. And I don't want to be a fig tree with nothing but leaves.

These scenes continually remind of the zeal of God for His house, His people, and His laws. Isn't it remarkable that Jesus quotes the Scriptures every time He faces the Pharisees or whenever He teaches something to His disciples? Not only did He know the Scriptures by heart, He knew how to apply them to every situation instantly without a moment's doubt.

When the chief priests and scribes opposed Jesus for accepting the praises of the children, Jesus responded:

> Have you never read, "From the lips of children and infants You have ordained praise"? (Matthew 21:16; cf. Psalm 8:2)

Moments before, with holy wrath, Jesus had exclaimed:

> It is written, . . . "My house will be called a house of prayer." (Matthew 21:13; cf. Isaiah 56:7)

The attitude of King Jesus always impresses me. I take joy in knowing that He is always near me, observing everything, and it comforts me to know that He is jealous of the things of God. I am one of the valued creatures of God, not because of what I might have done, but because of what Jesus has done for me. He made me a temple of the Holy Spirit, as He did all other believers (1 Corinthians 3:16). Of course, sometimes the King has to come with zeal and force to cleanse the temple again because I get it dirty so quickly, or I get involved in fruitless religious discussions instead of basing my arguments purely and exclusively on the Holy Scriptures, and every day I think and do things that offend God.

I still have a lot to learn from Jesus, but He is patient with me as He was with His first disciples, and as He is with all other members of His kingdom. I must say I feel honored that God has placed me in such a special kingdom. So I say:

> Blessed are You, Lord Jesus, Son of David!
>
> Blessed are You, King of the universe!

Read Matthew 21:12–17.

Think about Jesus' zeal for His Father's house.

What implications does Jesus' attitude have for your life?

Chapter 11

Part 1:
A Different Passover
(Matthew 26:17–29)

Every year, on the evening of the fourteenth day of the first month of the year, every Israelite family would kill a lamb or goat. It was the greatest shedding of animal blood on a single day! On the tenth day, the lambs and goats had been carefully chosen and kept until the celebration day of the great event: the Passover of the Lord.

Peter, James, and Thomas had been present at the killing of the lamb since their births and had eaten the Passover with their families every year. It was a great tradition!

Peter: It's different celebrating the Passover here in Jerusalem. When we were in Galilee, there weren't so many people.

Thomas: That's true. Here in Jerusalem, there are too many people, but I enjoy listening to their conversations and the family singing as they gather. There are children everywhere!

James: This place is beautiful. How did you think of preparing the Passover here?

Peter: The Teacher sent John and me to speak with the owner to see if we can meet here. I didn't think we would find an empty place in all Jerusalem, but Jesus always has resources. . . .

James: Of all the feasts we celebrate, this is the one I like the most. Maybe because it does me good to hear the story of how God liberated our ancestors from slavery in Egypt.

Thomas: I can't imagine the horror of the Egyptians that night when the angel of the Lord killed the oldest son of each family. That must have been terrible. Today we witness the death of many lambs, but *they* had to witness the death of their own sons. It must have been so painful!

James: What I remember most is how our grandfather told the story of the Passover. All the children in our family listened very carefully. He was very patient with us and answered our many questions. What always intrigued us was the fact that a lamb needed to be sacrificed to avoid death in the family. It was as if the poor innocent lamb paid for the sins of everyone in the house.

That was exactly God's plan: to keep His children, the ones He chose to be His people, from harm. That was the purpose of the lamb. That was the purpose of that great shedding of blood.

Jesus is in the Upper Room with His disciples, and just like Peter, James, and Thomas, He is looking back at old times. That's what the Passover is about, remembering old times. God's purpose when establishing this celebration was so that His people wouldn't forget what He had done for them when they were strangers and slaves. The Passover was a great tradition. What power God showed when He killed the Egyptians and passed over the Israelites! It was as if the blood painted on the doorposts had special powers—miraculous and supernatural powers to preserve life. What a fantastic story!

It is interesting how the Gospel writer Luke noted that when they were already eating the Passover, Jesus said to His disciples:

> I have eagerly desired to eat this Passover with you before I suffer. (Luke 22:15)

Few times, if ever, did Jesus express a desire. He is never heard to say "I want this" or "I want that." He always did what was necessary and not what He wished for. But the Passover was special. Jesus wanted to share it one last time with His disciples, those who belonged to His most intimate circle and who had been with Him in His ministry. Jesus Himself wanted to hear again the story of God's liberating power. He also wanted His disciples to be reassured by that story of liberation and power, because the events of the next few hours would make them stagger, as was demonstrated later that night.

But Jesus did something more, something unexpected and unique that had never been seen before at a Passover celebration: He changed the tradition. He put Himself in the place of the lamb. He would now shed His blood and paint the doorposts of the lives of the chosen ones so the angel of death could do them no harm. This is Jesus' last Passover supper and the first supper of the new covenant with the eternal Lamb. God had provided a very special Lamb for this Passover. From eternity He had chosen and preserved this Lamb for this occasion. His blood was not magic, but it was innocent and powerful; so powerful that its shedding secured the forgiveness of sins for all humanity for all time.

The Lord's Supper, Holy Communion, is the new Passover celebration where God passes over the sins of the people over and over and declares the people blameless. Jesus' disciples were beholding and participating in the new alliance that God was making with His people. Perhaps they didn't completely understand at the beginning. It's hard to leave such a strong, ancient tradition and begin a new one. But perhaps it didn't take them long to realize that the Lord's Supper was not a new tradition but the true fulfillment of the Passover. With the death of Jesus, the Passover Lamb, the cycle was completed and God's merciful attitude was confirmed as He passed over all our sins.

Jesus was so eager to leave this new alliance with His disciples! In this new covenant, Jesus includes not only His shed blood but also His own body so that He might remain present with His Church forever. Thus, Jesus makes His presence eternal and real every time we, His disciples, come together to celebrate the new Passover. It's God's plan for us to celebrate it frequently and to have the desire to eat in the company of other disciples.

We can't discount the whole atmosphere around the Passover festival: the lamb, the wine, the unleavened bread, the blessings, the story of the first Passover, singing psalms, and the prayers. God enriched this celebration with many details and specific instructions. It was the most important festival in the world! God Himself told Moses:

> This is a day you are to commemorate; for the generations to come you shall celebrate it as a festival to the Lord. (Exodus 12:14)

The first Christians in Corinth didn't understand the festive solemnity of the new Passover, and some not only got drunk, but they were disregarding others and not waiting to celebrate together in unity. The apostle Paul severely reprimanded that congregation because they did not understand that Jesus, the Passover Lamb, was among them.

The new Passover tradition that Jesus instituted is a permanent feast among Christians. Through this feast, we receive the eternal Lamb, in body and blood, and we hear again the solemn story of our liberation from our sins. Every Sunday, the Lord's Church, with songs and praises, psalms and solemn readings, says:

> "Oh, how I long to eat this Passover!"

Read Matthew 26:17–29.

Think about the most significant change Jesus made to the traditional Passover celebration.

Part 2:
Jesus Is Left Alone
(Matthew 26:36–46; 27:32–61)

The Passover celebration was part of Jesus' emotional and spiritual preparation to face God's judgment of sin and the angel of death that was coming to take His life. Now He is seen with His company on the Mount of Olives. From there He would see the soldiers and the mob of Jews coming with torches, spears, and weapons to come get Him. But that's not why Jesus was on the Mount of Olives; He went to be alone with His Father in prayer.

This was too difficult a moment to face alone. At other times, Jesus had spoken of the great joy produced by the Holy Spirit, but this was a moment of pure affliction.

> He took Peter and the two sons of Zebedee along with Him, and He began to be sorrowful and troubled. Then He said to them, "My soul is overwhelmed with sorrow to the point of death. Stay here and keep watch with Me." (Matthew 26:37–38)

But the disciples fell asleep. They left Him alone because they were too tired and didn't understand Jesus' anguish. Only Jesus knew what was happening inside Him. God's punishment of sin was getting closer, and Jesus was going to face that judgment alone with no one to defend Him. The disciples left Him to pray alone; then, when Jesus was arrested, they ran off, leaving Him in the hands of the soldiers and those who hated Him. And at the end, God Himself left Him alone; hence Jesus' cry from the cross:

> My God, My God, why have You forsaken Me? (Matthew 27:46)

This is the description of hell: loneliness and abandonment, suffering the unfair judgment of men and God's righteous judgment of sin.

What was the innocent Passover Lamb doing hanging on a cross? He was voluntarily taking the place of sinners—not only the place of one sinner, or a few sinners, but every sinner. According to Scripture, God punishes all sins, from the most terrible to those that seem to be the least important. Jesus went to the cross for the sins of everyone. He stained the cross with His blood so that when God would come to judge us, He would see the blood on the cross and pass by, doing us no harm. The apostle Paul, reflecting on the crucifixion and death of Jesus, says:

> For all have sinned and fall short of the glory of God, and are justified freely by His grace through the redemption that came by Christ Jesus. God presented Him as a sacrifice of atonement, through faith in His blood. He did this to demonstrate His justice, because in His forbearance He had left the sins committed beforehand unpunished. (Romans 3:23–25)

God's justice is manifested in two ways:

- Punishing sin with death; and
- Setting the sinner free from sin and death.

What a paradox! Those who offend God with their thoughts, words, and actions have freedom. There is no accusation of sin, no hard suffering forever, no loneliness, no death to hold us. We are free! The blood-stained cross is the doorway to liberty!

The angel of death respects the shed blood of the Lamb and does not harm us, but it didn't respect the Lamb. It didn't matter if the Lamb was innocent or if He had done any good in His life or had never sinned, or even if He was the very Son of God; the angel of death killed the Lamb with no mercy. What's more, before killing Him, he mocked, whipped, and laid on Him all manner of indescribable pain and suffering. He tore Him away from the presence of God and shamefully displayed Him to the world by crucifying Him along with evildoers. Then he buried Him in a tomb. The angel of death left the priests and teachers of the Law very happy, the Romans a little more at ease, and the disciples and the women who had accompanied Jesus to the very end distressed and hopeless.

Near the cross was Mary, Jesus' mother, desolate inside, deeply living Simeon's prophetic sentence pronounced when baby Jesus was presented at the temple.

> This child is destined to cause the falling and rising of many in Israel, and to be a sign that will be spoken against. . . . And a sword will pierce your own soul too. (Luke 2:34–35)

If Mary hadn't understand Simeon's words before, she definitely understood them now with all their depth and harshness.

Some of Jesus' disciples couldn't bear the scene. It was too sad to see how things were coming to an end. They had left their families and work to follow Jesus. They had hoped in Him. Even Peter had been ready to follow Him to the death—but when he saw the cross, he didn't think being recognized as Jesus' follower would be a good idea. From deep inside, he began cursing and swearing, saying, "I don't know the man!" (Matthew 26:74). Even the man who turned Jesus in, Judas Iscariot, was moved by the injustice of the judgment and tried to ease his conscience by returning the blood money he had been paid. But it didn't work. His repentance couldn't save Jesus' life, or his own.

There were graves that couldn't hold their dead (Matthew 27:52) and darkness that made the moment even more gloomy (v. 45). The earth itself could not stay still: it shook at the death of the Son of God (v. 51). The buildings of the Holy City were shaken to their foundations, to the point that:

> The curtain of the temple was torn in two from top to bottom. The earth shook and the rocks split. (Matthew 27:51)

What a magnificent signal God was sending to the world! The temple's curtain was an enormous tapestry (Exodus 26:31–37), and it separated the Holy of Holies from the Holy Place. The curtain's purpose was to prevent public access to the ark of the covenant that represented God's presence. Only the priest entered that holy place one time each year to offer the sacrifice and intercede for the people so that God might forgive their sins. With the tearing of the curtain, God was opening the door to His presence for all the people in the world. This was the first sign that God the Father had been satisfied with the expiatory sacrifice of Jesus. People could now enter into God's presence without needing a mediator (Hebrews 9) and without the necessity of propitiatory sacrifices. Because of His own Son's sacrifice, God receives us all before His throne. The author of the Letter written to the Hebrews says it in these words:

> When Christ came as high priest of the good things that are already here, He went through the greater and more perfect tabernacle. . . . He

> did not enter by means of the blood of goats and calves; but He entered the Most Holy Place once for all by His own blood, having obtained eternal redemption. . . . The blood of Christ . . . cleanse[s] our consciences from acts that lead to death, so that we may serve the living God! (Hebrews 9:11–12, 14)

So many things happened on that day! The temple curtain was torn in two, the sky was darkened, and the earth shook. People could be heard running and crying. There was no time to prepare for the Passover. Surely there were many who couldn't concentrate on the Passover story that night. The image of the crucified Master, first crying out, then absolutely silent, were deeply recorded in their minds. Joseph from Arimathea along with Nicodemus took Him down from the cross and placed Him in a tomb. The Son of God was buried in the cold, surrounded by silence and loneliness.

Read Matthew 27:32–61.

Think about the loneliness Jesus faced at the hour of His death.

Relate Jesus, the eternal Lamb of God, to the Passover lambs.

What does it mean to you that God gives you free access into His presence?

Part 3:
My Desire to Eat the Supper

During my early childhood, I carefully observed the ceremony of the celebration of Holy Communion. First of all, when we entered the church and saw the large number of people who came to the altar, we knew the worship service would be longer and maybe even more boring than usual because I didn't understand everything that went on. Besides, I was a little child and I couldn't participate. Holy Communion was only for the big people. The little ones just got to watch.

When the members of the church went to receive Communion, the men went first, in groups of four. When they were finished, the women followed, also in groups of four. Meanwhile, the rest of the congregation sang.

What fascinated me was the solemnity of the moment. There was nothing like it anywhere else. And one day, it was my turn. I was an adolescent and had been carefully instructed in the biblical teaching of the Eucharist. From that moment on, the Sundays when the Sacrament was celebrated were very special days to me.

Now, years later, I still experience the same solemnity, but now it is made richer by the experiences God has allowed me to live during every Communion. I know it isn't magic and that it has nothing to do with what I'm feeling or with the people around me. It has everything to do with Jesus' promise to be really present during that moment. That is what makes it solemn.

From ancient times, the Church understood the presence of Jesus in the Eucharist. When Christians from the first centuries gathered to celebrate the Sacrament of the Altar, they did it with great solemnity, following a carefully elaborated liturgy. The celebrant would say:

> Let grace come and let the world perish!

And the assembly answered:

> Hosanna to the Son of David!

Then the celebrant exclaimed:

> If any of you is holy, let him draw near; if not, let him do penitence! Maranatha!

And the congregation answered:

> Amen.

What is remarkable in this liturgical celebration is that the Early Church kept the Aramaic expression "Maranatha," which means, "Come, O Lord!"

At the end of his First Letter to the members of the Church at Corinth, the apostle Paul writes:

> If anyone does not love the Lord—a curse be on him. Come, O Lord! (1 Corinthians 16:22)

With this expression Paul warns everyone to be prepared for the Lord's coming. Although they don't know when the second coming will be, they do know that it is coming. This is the idea that the Early Church wanted to incorporate in the liturgy of Holy Communion, that Jesus will come again. Saying "Maranatha" is asking, "Come, O Lord!"

"Maranatha" is a confession of faith that God will come again, and a prayer that Jesus would speed His coming. The apostle Paul writes to the Church in Corinth:

> For whenever you eat this bread and drink this cup, you proclaim the Lord's death until He comes. (1 Corinthians 11:26)

It is certain that the Lord will come. And every time we celebrate the Eucharist, we are confessing to one another our faith in His second coming and our desire that Jesus would once and for all bring the kingdom of God to its final consummation.

But "Maranatha" is not just an expression of desire for the future. It also expresses a fervent desire that God would be present with us today: "Come, Lord, feed us with Your body and blood, forgive our sins, cleanse us now, give us Your peace."

We are not killing the Passover Lamb again. Jesus already died once for the sins of the people. Holy Communion is not a new sacrifice. On the contrary, it is a commemorative meal at which Jesus Himself is present through the bread and wine. Through the Eucharist, we commemorate what Jesus did for us and we celebrate our liberation. God doesn't take our sins into account; He strengthens our faith so we can continue facing our daily challenges.

In this new Passover supper, time is measured differently. In just one moment the past, present, and future all meet. During the administration of the Eucharist, we remember Jesus' past sufferings on the cross, His sacrifice as the Holy Lamb in our place. That is why Jesus orders:

> Do this, whenever you drink it, in remembrance of Me. (1 Corinthians 11:25)

We need to remember time and time again what God did for us and our inability to reconcile ourselves to God on our own, to heal ourselves, or to find peace and hope by our own means. Holy Communion reminds us of the sin that condemns us and binds us to a miserable life. That is why we include the confession of sins in the worship service, so we might be aware of our need for God.

"Do this in remembrance of Me. Remember that I sacrificed Myself for you. Now you're clean; you're forgiven. Now you can dare to live a life free of selfishness and fears. Now you can go the extra mile lightly, with joy," Jesus would say.

But it's not only the memory of His sacrifice that pushes us to a new life. It is the same Lord who makes Himself present in the moment we eat and drink the bread and wine. Jesus doesn't abandon us in the memory of His past sacrifice. He comes with all His reality, as King, as sovereign Lord, to be in the midst of His people. Now I understand the solemnity of the moment! Now I realize why this moment of Sunday worship has always been so special. It is because Jesus, the Lord of life and death, is present! Since I realized this, I cannot stop participating in the Eucharist. It is the most intense moment of the week. How could I let this pass? I am in the presence of the Lord, who personally comes to reaffirm the forgiveness He won on the cross. He comes to touch and heal me. Now my life has a new perspective. God elevates me to unforeseen dimensions. Everything else falls away. I am in the presence of the King.

Maranatha! Come, O Lord! In the Eucharist, we don't forget the future, the Lord who will come to judge and consummate the liberation of His people. This is how we remind one another that our lives are not just here and now, that God has plans for us to experience a much more glorious life, seated at the table with the Paschal Lamb, drinking new wine (Matthew 26:29).

Jesus celebrated Passover with His disciples, His new family. So also the Holy Communion is a family meal in which we are all equal in God's eyes and where everyone shares the same faith and hope. In this new Passover, God comes to be present in the midst of His family to encourage them and bravely proclaim the love that God has for a world that is falling apart. Holy Communion is a testimony that God has a people in this world and they have a great work to do: to add, one by one, more members to the great family of God.

Maranatha! Come, O Lord!

Read 1 Corinthians 11:23–26.

Discover the meaning of the Lord's Supper in this passage.

Chapter 12

Part 1:
Jesus Is Unstoppable

Death can leave a bitter taste in the mouth and a rage that is hard to contain because there is nothing you can do about it. When people are dead, they're dead. You can't go back in time to avoid the accident, or stop time to look for more medical options. Death rips our loved ones from our side, never to return. So we cry because there is emptiness inside that no one else can fill.

Thomas was probably angry with Jesus because He didn't look for a way to avoid His crucifixion. Now Thomas had hardened his heart and didn't want to believe anything the other disciples told him; he declared:

> Unless I see the nail marks in His hands and put my finger where the nails were, and put my hand into His side, I will not believe it. (John 20:25)

His decision was final and was supported by past experience: dead people don't come back to life!

Several times, Jesus had said:

> "The Son of Man is going to be betrayed into the hands of men. They will kill Him, and after three days He will rise." But [the disciples] did not understand what He meant and were afraid to ask Him about it. (Mark 9:31–32)

When the word *death*, our insurmountable enemy, is mentioned, it fills us with fear and we don't think to ask questions. Thomas didn't ask:

- Where did you see Him?
- How was He?
- Whom did He look like?
- What did He say?
- Will He appear again?

Thomas's mind and heart were overwhelmed, unable to think, reflect, or even remember that Jesus had raised Lazarus from the dead! There's no doubt in Thomas. He firmly believes that Jesus is dead.

The incredulity of the other disciples was no different. When the women said they had seen Jesus alive, "they did not believe the women, because their words seemed to them like nonsense" (Luke 24:11). But Peter went running to see for himself. Perhaps out of all the disciples, he was the most eager to find out about Jesus. Death had robbed Peter of the opportunity to ask Jesus' forgiveness for having failed Him the night of His trial. That's what death does: it cuts off all possibilities and dreams. Death sometimes erases God's promises from the memory and brings into the light feelings of guilt, fear, and insecurity. It is worthy to note that when the women went to the tomb that Sunday morning, the angel told them:

> "Remember how He told you, while He was still with you in Galilee: 'The Son of Man must be delivered into the hands of sinful men, be crucified and on the third day be raised again.'" Then they remembered His words. When they came back from the tomb, they told all these things to the Eleven and to all the others. (Luke 24:6–9)

Here is the difference. The resurrection of Jesus casts light on all His promises. Now everything has another dimension. It took the disciples some time to get used to this new reality. They were both happy and fearful at the same time and for several reasons. Jesus was with them again. It had not been in vain that they left everything to follow Him. And death! Death was now defeated forever! The last and greatest enemy of God's creation had been conquered forever!

"My Lord and my God!" exclaimed Thomas (John 20:28). He was astonished that the scars were still present and yet could not keep Jesus under the dominion of death. Thomas didn't want to see another messiah sent from heaven. He wanted to see the same One who had been crucified, the One who had made such an impact in his life. And he saw Him! Now the impact was even greater.

Jesus took the time to show Himself alive to the women and to explain to His two disciples on their way to Emmaus that everything that had happened to the Messiah was predicted in Scripture (Luke 24:13–27). He also approached Peter with infinite tenderness and not a single reproach to restore him three times while they were having breakfast at the beach (John 21:15–17).

The resurrection left the disciples perplexed and joyful. It left the Pharisees and chief priests disturbed and worried. Surely, now that the word of His resurrection was becoming more public, Jesus' enemies needed to find the body. If they could just find the dead body of Jesus, they would be able to keep His followers quiet. But it was not possible to find the dead body because the Lord was indeed alive and active, reassuring His followers that He had indeed conquered death.

Before ascending to heaven, Jesus wanted to remove all doubt from the hearts of the disciples with regard to His resurrection. The Gospel writer Mark points out:

> Later Jesus appeared to the Eleven as they were eating; He rebuked them for their lack of faith and their stubborn refusal to believe those who had seen Him after He had risen. (Mark 16:14)

Only the resurrection gives the ministry and death of Jesus its meaning. That God raised Him from the dead is a resounding proof that He was satisfied with the saving work of Jesus. The resurrection of Jesus is everything. The apostle Paul understood this concept perfectly and based his entire theology, outlined in his epistles, squarely on the resurrection of Jesus. He writes to the Corinthians:

> And if Christ has not been raised, your faith is futile; you are still in your sins. . . . If only for this life we have hope in Christ, we are to be pitied more than all men. (1 Corinthians 15:17, 19)

What makes Jesus' resurrection the central point of the story of salvation is that it affects both the temporal and eternal life of believers, because just as Jesus rose, we will also rise in glory.

> But Christ has indeed been raised from the dead, the firstfruits of those who have fallen

> asleep. . . . For as in Adam all die, so in Christ all will be made alive. (1 Corinthians 15:20, 22)

Once again this shows that everything God does is for the benefit of His creatures. The death and resurrection of Jesus are not isolated events, but rather powerful events planned from all eternity, and events that still have an effect today. The apostle Paul expresses it this way:

> But whatever was to my profit I now consider loss for the sake of Christ. What is more, I consider everything a loss compared to the surpassing greatness of knowing Christ Jesus my Lord, for whose sake I have lost all things. I consider them rubbish, that I may gain Christ. . . . I want to know Christ and the power of His resurrection. (Philippians 3:7–8, 10)

And to the Romans, he explains:

> We were therefore buried with Him through baptism into death in order that, just as Christ was raised from the dead through the glory of the Father, we too may live a new life. (Romans 6:4)

The resurrection of Jesus changes our lives; it invigorates, energizes, and fills us with hope in the face of our own death. God uses the same power in us that He used to raise Jesus. How well He treats us! With the power He used to return Jesus to life, He gives us a new life. God is extraordinarily generous. He placed Jesus on the cross in our place. He didn't allow the pain of crucifixion and death to fall on us. He doesn't share His suffering with us. He only shares the power of Jesus' victorious resurrection.

Read Matthew 28:1–10.

Observe what happened to the guards.

How did the women react?

What was spectacular about the appearance of the angel?

What were Jesus' first words?

Part 2:
The Exaltation of Jesus Christ

The Gospel writers' description of Jesus' ascension is concise. Absolutely simple. There are hardly any details about this glorious event. Actually, the components of this story are the same as those in the other great events in Jesus' life: angels and surprised people. At Jesus' birth, the angels appeared to explain to the shepherds what was happening. At His resurrection, the angels moved the stone and told the women about what had just happened. Now, at the ascension, the angels redirected the disciples' gaze, so they wouldn't stay frozen in amazement, and reaffirmed His promise:

> This same Jesus, who has been taken from you into heaven, will come back in the same way you have seen Him go into heaven. (Acts 1:11)

The intervention of the angels adds a heavenly element to these events because they are of great importance for humanity and because they needed a true explanation that no human could give. God had to leave the fact well established that Jesus "had been taken from [them]." From now on, there would be no more amazing appearances. Jesus wouldn't walk through any more walls or doors. He wouldn't surprise them on the beach with miraculous catches of fish (John 21). They would not see Him again.

This is how simple the story of the ascension of Jesus is:

> After He said this, He was taken up before their very eyes, and a cloud hid Him from their sight. (Acts 1:9)

There are no more details.

God chose to raise Jesus to heaven in front of only His most intimate disciples. After His resurrection Jesus chose to show Himself only to those who had believed His Word. If Jesus had ascended in the middle of Jerusalem in front of everyone, including the Pharisees and interpreters of the Law, it would have caused a great commotion since most of them would not have understood and would have become even more confused.

The visible ascension of Jesus made sense to those who had received the promise:

> In My Father's house are many rooms; if it were not so, I would have told you. I am going there to prepare a place for you. And if I go and prepare a place for you, I will come back and take you to be with Me that you also may be where I am. (John 14:2–3)

God took Jesus from the view of the disciples so they would start looking at Him with their faith and not with their eyes. Heaven is His exaltation, the place from which He will reign and make Himself present in all places at all times. Peter and John testified boldly in the temple after being freed from jail by an angel: "God exalted Him to His own right hand as Prince and Savior that He might give repentance and forgiveness of sins to Israel" (Acts 5:31).

The whole Church, since the first centuries, confessed her faith with the words of the Apostles' Creed, saying:

> He ascended into heaven and sits at the right hand of God the Father Almighty. From thence He will come to judge the living and the dead.

This confession of faith is based on some key passages of the New Testament. For example, the apostle Paul sums up the theology of Jesus' ascension with these words:

> Therefore God exalted Him to the highest place and gave Him the name that is above every name, that at the name of Jesus every knee should bow, in heaven and on earth and under the earth, and every tongue confess that Jesus Christ is Lord, to the glory of God the Father. (Philippians 2:9–11)

When the same apostle writes to the Thessalonians for the second time, he comforts them in their persecutions, saying that God will "give relief to you who are troubled, and to us as well. This will happen when the Lord Jesus is revealed from heaven in blazing fire with His powerful angels" (2 Thessalonians 1:7).

Meanwhile, we have a simple description of the ascension of Jesus and His return. It cannot be doubted that Jesus will return again among clouds, fire, and trumpets. It will be a glorious day that Christians should always keep in mind. Until this takes place, Jesus is interceding for us before the Father (Hebrews 9:24), and is preparing a place for us. I can't imagine a better place for the children of God than there in the highest heavenly places with those who have been washed in the blood of the Lamb.

> Never again will they hunger; never again will they thirst. The sun will not beat upon them, nor any scorching heat. For the Lamb at the center of the throne will be their shepherd; He will lead them to springs of living water. And God will wipe away every tear from their eyes. (Revelation 7:16–17)

What a masterful description John makes here of the place where Jesus is, preparing a place for us. And yet He never stops being among us today, here, in our circumstances. Jesus ascended in order to move out of our sight and to leave this physical world where we are restricted to a determined time and place. Jesus is now in another world, in a different dimension, from where He can exercise His power over the entire human race. There is no space that Jesus cannot fill now. He is present among His people every time His Word is read and Baptism and Holy Communion are administered. He makes Himself present wherever there are two or three gathered in His name (Matthew 18:20). The Holy Spirit that Jesus sent from the Father to all His disciples after His ascension is still here, extremely active, bringing Jesus to the people to forgive their sins, strengthen their faith, and encourage them to live life according to the new way He taught them.

It is worth noting how Luke describes what the disciples did after Jesus ascended:

> Then they worshiped Him and returned to Jerusalem with great joy. And they stayed continually at the temple, praising God. (Luke 24:52–53)

Isn't it interesting that after Jesus left them, the disciples didn't miss their Teacher? They didn't grieve His parting or ask Him to stay with them. There was no sadness or reproach because of His ascension. Undoubtedly, Jesus didn't leave His disciples empty; He left them with His promise to be with them always, until the ends of the earth, and He filled their hearts with joy and peace. Several times the Book of the Acts of the Apostles says that the disciples were filled with joy and the Holy Spirit (Acts 13:52).

The presence of the Holy Spirit after Pentecost supplied all the support, guidance, and comfort they needed. Suddenly, Jesus' promises were made real in the hearts of the disciples:

> And I will ask the Father, and He will give you another Counselor to be with you forever. . . . I will not leave you as orphans; I will come to you. (John 14:16, 18)

Since His physical departure, Jesus is always present in His Church. This is why one of the marks of the Church is joy in the Holy Spirit. The world cannot see Jesus or experience the joy that only God can give. The Church, however, can see, experience, and, even more important, share this joy with a world that is blind, orphaned, and sad.

God provides the power and joy so that, under His Lordship, we might testify to His love for the whole human race.

For this reason, Jesus concludes His earthly ministry with these words:

> But you will receive power when the Holy Spirit comes on you; and you will be My witnesses in Jerusalem, and in all Judea and Samaria, and to the ends of the earth. (Acts 1:8)

Read Acts 1:1–11.

What did Jesus do during the forty days between His resurrection and ascension?

Notice how many promises there are in this passage.

How do these promises affect you?

What differences do the promises of Jesus and the angels make in your life?

Part 3:
Cemetery Stories

When I was a child, my father used to take me around on his old motorcycle. When my brother tagged along with us, he would get the backseat because he was the oldest, and I would ride on top of the fuel tank. From there I had a good view of the whole road.

My dad was a pastor who served in three rural congregations plus the biggest congregation in the town where we lived. I enjoyed going to these places with him. I had friends my age; we rode horses together, and there was always good food. But I didn't like it when there was a funeral. I did everything in my power to avoid the cemetery. If anyone close to our family died, I would attend the funeral because my conscience wouldn't allow me to stay home, but later on, I would suffer the consequences. At night, I couldn't sleep; I dreamed about caskets, tombs, and evil spirits. There was a time during my childhood when tombs and dead people frightened me. I think I heard too many cemetery stories.

When Jesus was crucified and buried, the chief priests and Pharisees invented an "incredible" story about the cemetery. That story has two parts. The first is when they go to see Pilate and say:

> "Sir," they said, "we remember that while He was still alive that deceiver said, 'After three days I will rise again.' So give the order for the tomb to be made secure until the third day. Otherwise, His disciples may come and steal the body and tell the people that He has been

> raised from the dead. This last deception will be worse than the first." (Matthew 27:63–64)

The Pharisees and chief priests were not at peace, even after killing Jesus. Somehow they knew that all this business about Jesus of Nazareth wasn't finished. Therefore, they invented a ridiculous story to convince Pilate to secure the tomb. Secure a tomb! Who would have thought of that? What would happen if the disciples decided to steal Jesus' body? Nothing! The disciples weren't exactly dangerous. All of them ran off when they saw the soldiers coming the night Jesus was arrested. The disciples weren't going to do anything. They were locked inside a house, sad and disillusioned.

But the truth is that the Pharisees and chief priests were not calm, nor were they sure what might happen after the crucifixion of Jesus. They tried to stop God with the governor's help by securing the stone in front of the tomb and adding Roman soldiers there to guard it.

The second part of the story is when the Pharisees and chief priests put their emergency plan into action since the first plan failed to work. This plan consisted of a big lie and a good bribe. They knew they couldn't bribe the soldiers with just a little money because if the soldiers were to get caught, they would be dishonored and sent someplace even less desirable than Jerusalem. Therefore:

> When the chief priests had met with the elders and devised a plan, they gave the soldiers a large sum of money, telling them, "You are to say, 'His disciples came during the night and stole Him away while we were asleep.'" (Matthew 28:12–13)

The second plan of Jesus' enemies was even more ridiculous than the first. How could soldiers who were sleeping all night be good witnesses? If they had been asleep, they couldn't have seen a thing. At night, cemeteries are "silent as a tomb." I can't imagine that the disciples could have arrived at the tomb and silently removed the heavy stone without making any noise, all in front of trained Roman guards.

I admire the imagination of the Pharisees and chief priests for inventing this story, and I deplore their sinful attitude. What I like about all this is that it didn't matter how important the relationship was between the religious leaders and the governor, or the amount of money they used to bribe the soldiers, or how imaginative their cemetery stories were. They couldn't stop Jesus.

God is unstoppable. He keeps loving us and looking after us. There is no political power, no bribe money, no horror stories that can keep Jesus from coming over and over to meet with those He loves.

But what I like most about this whole story is the attitude of Jesus. After His resurrection, He didn't bother to return to the Pharisees and chief priests to show them that He was right. It would have been easy to surprise them at breakfast and say, "Look, here I am, just like I said. You were wrong, I was right!"

In fact, Jesus did the complete opposite. He went to those who loved Him, the ones who were sad about His death and fearful of everyone else. He appeared first to the women and later to the rest of His followers. The apostle Paul says that Jesus appeared to more that five hundred brothers and sisters at one time (1 Corinthians 15:6). Jesus invested His time in them, demonstrating that He was still focused on His mission. Jesus didn't come to show off to the religious leaders that He was right, but to love those who belonged to Him. Jesus didn't allow the Pharisees, the governor, or the Roman army to sidetrack His mission. He had other things to do.

Jesus went to see Thomas, who needed a more convincing proof of His resurrection. What impresses me about this encounter with Thomas is that Jesus showed him His wounds. It never would have occurred to me that a glorified body, ready to ascend to heaven, would still carry with it the scars of earthly wounds. What's more, I am amazed to see how these scars served as a testimony for the doubting Thomas.

This makes me think about my own wounds, the ones I keep collecting year after year and that leave me scarred. There are wounds that I received from others when they betrayed me and took advantage of my honesty, or when they lied to gain some personal benefit. I have other scars that I gave myself every time I fell into sin. If all those scars could be seen on my body, I would look disfigured! But I thank God that His love has healed all of my wounds. I know I have scars, but I know they serve as a testimony to others about the power of God and the care that He has for His children.

At the end, Jesus returned to His Father. It does me good to know that He is preparing a place for me, because I know no one else can do it better. Here, I often feel out of place because some people take my place, or I'm too blind to see the place that God has provided for me to live a plentiful life. In heaven, this won't happen. There I will have a glorious place along with all the redeemed.

But Jesus is not only preparing a place for us. From heaven, He governs His Church, of which I am a part. When the heavenly Father set Him at His right hand:

> God exalted Him to the highest place and gave Him the name that is above every name, that at the name of Jesus every knee should bow, in heaven and on earth and under the earth, and every tongue confess that Jesus Christ is Lord,

> to the glory of God the Father. (Philippians 2:9–11)

It is my prayer that everyone who has read this book will recognize and confess that Jesus of Nazareth is the Lord, to the glory of God the Father.

Read Matthew 27:62–66 and 28:11–15.

Reflect on the fear of the Pharisees and chief priests, and on the lies they told about the resurrection of Jesus.

Read John 20:26–28.

Think of a wound Jesus has healed in you, and that today serves as a testimony of God's love before others.